Artificial Intelligence and Climate Change: Using AI to Support Renewable Energy, Reduce Emissions, Manage Water, Enhance Food Systems, Improve Disaster Response, and Drive Adaptation

1

Copyright

Artificial Intelligence and Climate Change: Using AI to Support Renewable Energy, Reduce Emissions, Manage Water, Enhance Food Systems, Improve Disaster Response, and Drive Adaptation

ISBN (eBook): 978-1-991368-07-2

ISBN (Paperback): 978-1-991368-08-9

Published by Global Climate Solutions

First Edition, 2025

Cover design and interior layout by Global Climate Solutions

Table of Contents

Introduction

The world stands at a critical juncture, confronted by the escalating impacts of climate change. Rising global temperatures, increasingly erratic weather patterns, and widespread environmental degradation are placing immense strain on natural systems and societies worldwide. At the same time, the digital revolution is transforming every sector of the global economy, offering new tools and pathways to address complex challenges. The convergence of these two megatrends—climate change and digital technology—presents an unprecedented opportunity to reimagine how humanity adapts to and mitigates the climate crisis.

Artificial intelligence (AI) lies at the heart of this digital opportunity. With its ability to process vast datasets, recognize patterns, and make predictions at a speed and scale impossible for humans alone, AI is reshaping the landscape of climate action. From optimizing renewable energy systems and improving agricultural practices to monitoring deforestation and supporting disaster response, AI is already beginning to play a transformative role. Its potential to accelerate innovation, improve decision-making, and enable more efficient resource management makes it a key enabler in the fight against climate change.

Before delving further, it is important to clarify several key terms. Adaptation refers to adjustments in natural or human systems to moderate harm or exploit beneficial opportunities from actual or expected climate effects. Mitigation focuses on efforts to reduce or prevent the emission of greenhouse gases, aiming to limit the magnitude of future climate change. AI is a branch of computer science that enables machines to perform tasks that typically require human intelligence, such as learning, reasoning, and problem-solving. Throughout this book, these definitions will guide our exploration of how AI intersects with both climate adaptation and mitigation.

This book is structured to provide a comprehensive overview of the intersections between AI and climate change solutions. Following a concise introduction, the chapters examine the foundations of AI in climate action, delve into sector-specific applications for both mitigation and adaptation, explore policy and governance implications, discuss key challenges and risks, and conclude with a look toward the future. The text aims to offer clarity on concepts, highlight technological opportunities, and underscore the importance of ethical and responsible approaches to AI deployment in climate contexts.

A deliberate choice has been made to focus on principles, frameworks, and applications, rather than specific case studies or project examples. This approach provides a broad and foundational understanding, allowing readers to grasp the essential strategies, challenges, and possibilities without being limited by the context of particular regions or organizations. By centering on generalizable knowledge, this book is intended to serve as a practical guide for policymakers, professionals, researchers, and students seeking to leverage AI for effective and responsible climate action.

Chapter 1: The Climate Challenge and the Digital Revolution

Chapter 1 introduces the urgent and complex challenge of climate change and the pivotal role that digital innovation now plays in shaping society's response. As the planet faces rising temperatures, more frequent extreme weather events, and mounting pressures on natural systems, the need for effective adaptation and mitigation has never been greater. At the same time, the digital revolution—marked by advances in computing, connectivity, AI, and data analytics—is transforming the way individuals, businesses, and governments operate. These two global forces are converging, offering unprecedented opportunities to address climate risks with new tools, smarter strategies, and more collaborative approaches. This chapter sets the stage by exploring the causes and impacts of climate change, introducing the foundational concepts of adaptation and mitigation, and examining how digital transformation and AI are reshaping the possibilities for climate action. Together, these themes highlight the promise and responsibility of leveraging digital technology for a sustainable future.

1.1 Understanding Climate Change: Causes and Impacts

Climate change is widely recognized as one of the most pressing challenges facing humanity today. At its core, climate change refers to long-term shifts in global or regional climate patterns, particularly those changes observed since the late 19th century as a result of increased levels of atmospheric greenhouse gases. These changes are driven primarily by human activities such as the burning of fossil fuels—including coal, oil, and natural gas—for energy, transportation, and industry. The combustion of these fuels releases significant quantities of carbon dioxide (CO_2) and other greenhouse gases (GHGs), which trap heat in the Earth's atmosphere and lead to the warming of the planet.

Beyond fossil fuel use, other major contributors to climate change include deforestation, agriculture, and various industrial processes. Deforestation reduces the planet's capacity to absorb CO_2, while agricultural practices can release methane (CH_4) and nitrous oxide (N_2O), both of which are potent GHGs. Industrial processes can emit a range of additional GHGs, further intensifying the greenhouse effect. The accumulation of these gases in the atmosphere disrupts the Earth's energy balance, leading to changes in temperature, precipitation patterns, and weather extremes.

The impacts of climate change are both widespread and profound. Average global temperatures have risen, resulting in more frequent and severe heatwaves, prolonged droughts, and the increased melting of glaciers and polar ice. Sea levels are rising due to thermal expansion and melting ice sheets, threatening coastal communities with flooding and erosion. Changing precipitation patterns are affecting water resources, agriculture, and biodiversity, while more intense storms and hurricanes are leading to increased damage to infrastructure and livelihoods.

In addition to environmental impacts, climate change poses significant risks to human health, food security, and economic stability. Heat-related illnesses, the spread of vector-borne diseases, and reduced agricultural productivity threaten vulnerable populations around the world. The loss of biodiversity and ecosystem services further compounds these challenges, undermining the resilience of both natural and human systems.

Understanding the causes and impacts of climate change is essential for developing effective strategies for both mitigation—addressing the root causes by reducing GHG emissions—and adaptation—responding to the impacts and building resilience in the face of inevitable change. As the scientific consensus on climate change has grown stronger, so too has the recognition of the urgent need for coordinated, global action that leverages innovation and technology to safeguard our planet for current and future generations.

1.2 Adaptation vs. Mitigation: Key Strategies

In responding to the challenge of climate change, two main strategies have emerged: adaptation and mitigation. These approaches, while distinct, are both essential for building a resilient and sustainable future.

Mitigation refers to efforts aimed at addressing the root causes of climate change by reducing greenhouse gas emissions or enhancing the capacity of sinks to absorb these gases. Key mitigation strategies include increasing energy efficiency, transitioning to renewable energy sources such as solar and wind, promoting sustainable land use and forestry practices, and advancing low-carbon technologies across sectors. Mitigation also encompasses actions such as improving waste management, supporting the circular economy, and adopting cleaner transportation systems. By reducing the concentration of greenhouse gases in the atmosphere, mitigation seeks to limit the magnitude of future climate change and prevent the most severe potential impacts.

Adaptation, on the other hand, focuses on adjusting natural and human systems in response to current or expected climate impacts. Adaptation strategies aim to reduce vulnerability, minimize damage, and harness potential opportunities created by changing climate conditions. These strategies include strengthening infrastructure to withstand extreme weather, developing drought- or flood-resistant crops, managing water resources more efficiently, enhancing early warning systems, and protecting coastal areas from sea-level rise. Adaptation measures can be proactive—anticipating and preparing for future risks—or reactive, responding to events as they occur.

While mitigation tackles the causes of climate change, adaptation addresses its effects. The most effective climate action combines both strategies, recognizing that some degree of change is unavoidable even as efforts are made to reduce emissions. Integrating adaptation and mitigation creates synergies, builds resilience, and maximizes benefits for communities, economies, and the environment. Understanding and applying both approaches is fundamental to a comprehensive response to climate change.

1.3 The Digital Transformation of Society

The rapid digital transformation of society over the past few decades has reshaped the way individuals, organizations, and governments interact, communicate, and solve problems. Advances in computing power, connectivity, and data analytics have given rise to a new era where digital technologies are deeply embedded in daily life and critical infrastructure. From smartphones and smart sensors to cloud computing and the Internet of Things (IoT), digital tools have revolutionized information sharing, decision-making, and service delivery across sectors.

This ongoing digital revolution has also expanded the ability to gather, process, and analyze unprecedented volumes of data in real time. Technologies such as remote sensing, machine learning (ML), and advanced modeling provide detailed insights into complex systems—whether monitoring weather patterns, managing energy consumption, or tracking the health of ecosystems. These innovations not only enhance our understanding of global challenges like climate change but also equip decision-makers with actionable intelligence to respond swiftly and effectively.

Moreover, the digital transformation is driving collaboration and innovation on a global scale. Open data platforms, digital marketplaces, and online communities enable the exchange of knowledge and best practices across borders. Digitalization fosters the development of new business models and governance frameworks, while also making advanced tools more accessible to communities and individuals who previously lacked such resources.

However, the integration of digital technologies is not without challenges. Issues related to digital equity, data privacy, and cybersecurity have emerged as pressing concerns, requiring thoughtful governance and robust safeguards. Despite these challenges, the digital transformation presents vast opportunities for addressing the complexities of climate change. By harnessing the power of data and AI, society can build smarter, more resilient systems that are better equipped to adapt to—and mitigate—the impacts of a changing climate.

1.4 What is Artificial Intelligence? Definitions and Types

AI is a branch of computer science focused on developing systems and technologies capable of performing tasks that typically require human intelligence. At its core, AI is about creating machines and algorithms that can learn from data, recognize patterns, make decisions, and solve problems—sometimes with minimal or no human intervention. The field of AI encompasses a wide range of approaches, methods, and levels of complexity, all aimed at replicating or augmenting aspects of human cognition.

Definitions of AI can vary depending on context, but most agree that AI systems possess the ability to sense their environment, process information, and act in ways that achieve specific goals. Unlike traditional computer programs that follow explicit step-by-step instructions, AI systems can improve their performance over time by learning from new data and adapting to changing circumstances. This capacity for learning and adaptation is what distinguishes AI from conventional automation.

There are several major types of AI, each with unique capabilities and applications. Narrow AI (or Weak AI) refers to systems designed to perform a specific task, such as recognizing faces in photographs, recommending products online, or predicting weather patterns. These systems are highly specialized and do not possess general reasoning abilities beyond their programmed functions. In contrast, General AI (or Strong AI) describes hypothetical systems with cognitive abilities comparable to those of humans, able to perform any intellectual task a person can. While General AI remains a theoretical concept, Narrow AI is widely used in practical applications today.

Within Narrow AI, ML is the most prevalent subfield. ML involves training algorithms to identify patterns in data and make predictions or decisions without being explicitly programmed for each possible scenario. Examples include supervised learning, where models are trained on labeled datasets; unsupervised learning, which identifies patterns in unlabeled data; and reinforcement learning, where systems learn through trial and error.

Another rapidly evolving branch is Deep Learning, a subset of ML that uses multi-layered artificial neural networks to process complex data such as images, speech, and natural language. Deep learning has driven major advances in areas like image recognition, voice assistants, and autonomous vehicles.

AI also includes rule-based systems, expert systems, natural language processing, robotics, and computer vision. As these technologies evolve, they are increasingly integrated into solutions for climate adaptation and mitigation, supporting data analysis, forecasting, optimization, and decision-making in diverse sectors. Understanding the definitions and types of AI is crucial for leveraging its potential in tackling the climate crisis.

1.5 How AI Amplifies Climate Response

AI is transforming the way societies approach climate change by enabling faster, more precise, and more adaptive responses to both mitigation and adaptation challenges. By processing massive volumes of data from diverse sources—such as satellites, sensors, and remote monitoring devices—AI can reveal patterns and trends that would be difficult or impossible for humans to detect alone. This data-driven insight empowers decision-makers to anticipate risks, allocate resources more efficiently, and tailor interventions to specific environmental conditions.

One significant way AI amplifies climate response is through the optimization of complex systems. For example, AI algorithms can balance the supply and demand of renewable energy in real time, making it easier to integrate solar and wind power into electricity grids. These systems learn from historical and live data, adjusting operations automatically to minimize waste, reduce emissions, and ensure reliable power delivery. Similarly, AI can help industries identify inefficiencies in manufacturing or supply chains, driving down resource use and greenhouse gas emissions through process improvements that would be difficult to achieve manually.

AI also enhances climate adaptation efforts by supporting more accurate forecasting and early warning systems. ML models can predict extreme weather events, such as floods, droughts, or heatwaves, with increasing accuracy, allowing governments and communities to prepare in advance and reduce harm. In agriculture, AI-driven tools analyze soil conditions, weather forecasts, and crop health to recommend optimal planting times, irrigation schedules, and pest management practices, supporting resilience in the face of climate variability.

Another important contribution of AI is its ability to automate monitoring and compliance. By analyzing satellite images, sensor data, and other information streams, AI can detect illegal deforestation, monitor emissions from power plants, and ensure compliance with environmental regulations in near real time. This enhances transparency, accountability, and the effectiveness of climate policies.

Despite its power, AI is not a standalone solution. Its effectiveness depends on the availability of high-quality data, thoughtful integration with human expertise, and a strong ethical framework to guide its development and use. When applied responsibly, AI offers a powerful set of tools that can accelerate climate action, improve resilience, and help society navigate the complexities of a changing planet.

1.6 Barriers and Risks in Digital-Climate Integration

While AI and digital technologies offer enormous potential for advancing climate change mitigation and adaptation, several barriers and risks can limit their effectiveness and even create new challenges. One major barrier is data quality and availability. AI systems require large amounts of accurate, timely, and representative data to function effectively. In many regions, especially low-income or remote areas, reliable climate, environmental, and socioeconomic data may be scarce or inaccessible, reducing the effectiveness of digital solutions.

Another barrier is the digital divide. Not all communities, organizations, or countries have equal access to advanced technologies, high-speed internet, or the technical expertise needed to implement AI-driven climate tools. This gap risks leaving vulnerable populations further behind, potentially worsening existing inequalities. Addressing these disparities requires targeted investments in digital infrastructure, capacity building, and education.

There are also important ethical and governance risks. AI models can unintentionally reinforce biases present in the underlying data or in their design, leading to unfair or discriminatory outcomes. Questions around data privacy and security are heightened as more personal and sensitive information is collected and analyzed. Additionally, the transparency and explainability of AI algorithms are critical for building trust, especially when these systems are used in public decision-making or to enforce regulations.

Another risk is the energy footprint of AI itself. Training and running complex AI models can require significant computational power and electricity, contributing to emissions if not managed sustainably. There is also the potential for technology misuse or unintended consequences, where digital tools are deployed without adequate safeguards or oversight.

Recognizing and addressing these barriers and risks is essential for realizing the full potential of digital technologies in climate response. Careful governance, robust ethical standards, and a commitment to inclusion and equity are all necessary to ensure that AI supports—not undermines—progress toward a more resilient and sustainable future.

1.7 Chapter Summary

This chapter introduced the urgent challenge of climate change and highlighted the transformative role of AI in society's response. It explained the fundamental drivers and impacts of climate change, emphasizing the distinction between adaptation and mitigation as the two pillars of climate action. The chapter described how the digital transformation of society has created new opportunities for data-driven solutions, collaboration, and innovation, making it possible to address climate complexities at unprecedented scale and speed.

The basics of AI were clarified, including its definitions, main types, and how it differs from traditional automation. The discussion then explored the ways AI amplifies climate response—by improving forecasting, optimizing resource use, and supporting better decision-making in areas such as energy, agriculture, and disaster preparedness. However, several barriers and risks were also identified, such as issues of data quality, the digital divide, ethical concerns, and the environmental impact of digital infrastructure.

Overall, this chapter laid the foundation for understanding the intersection of AI and climate change. As the book progresses, it will explore the practical applications of AI in different sectors, discuss governance and ethical considerations, and provide a roadmap for responsibly leveraging digital technologies in the pursuit of climate resilience and sustainability.

Chapter 2: Foundations of AI for Climate Action

Chapter 2 lays the groundwork for understanding how AI can be harnessed in the global response to climate change. As AI rapidly evolves and becomes embedded in many aspects of daily life and decision-making, it is critical to clarify the core concepts, types, and requirements of AI in the climate context. This chapter introduces the main categories of AI—including ML, deep learning, and data analytics—and explains how they are applied to analyze complex climate data, model uncertainty, and support risk management. Key considerations such as data quality, access to climate data sources, and the challenges of integrating AI into climate solutions are examined in detail. Ethical issues and principles for responsible AI development are addressed, emphasizing transparency, fairness, and collaboration. By establishing these foundational elements, the chapter prepares readers to explore the practical applications, opportunities, and limitations of AI as a tool for effective and equitable climate action.

2.1 AI Types: ML, Deep Learning, Data Analytics

AI is a broad field made up of several distinct but interconnected approaches. Three of the most important for climate change adaptation and mitigation are ML, deep learning, and data analytics. Understanding their unique characteristics and applications is essential for recognizing how AI can drive effective climate solutions.

ML is a subset of AI that enables computer systems to learn from data and improve their performance over time without being explicitly programmed for every task. Instead of following fixed instructions, ML algorithms analyze large datasets, identify patterns, and make predictions or decisions based on those patterns. There are several types of ML, including supervised learning (where the algorithm is trained on labeled data), unsupervised learning (where it looks for patterns in unlabeled data), and reinforcement learning (where it learns through trial and error in an interactive environment). In climate applications, ML is used for tasks like forecasting weather events, predicting crop yields, and detecting anomalies in energy grids.

Deep learning is an advanced subset of ML that relies on artificial neural networks with many layers—hence the term "deep." These neural networks are inspired by the human brain's structure and are especially well-suited for handling large volumes of complex, unstructured data such as images, audio, or text. Deep learning has powered breakthroughs in fields like image recognition, speech processing, and natural language understanding. For climate action, deep learning is used to interpret satellite imagery, model extreme weather, and automate the detection of deforestation or changes in land use with impressive accuracy.

Data analytics refers to the systematic process of collecting, processing, and analyzing data to extract useful insights and support decision-making. While not unique to AI, data analytics is a crucial enabler of AI-driven solutions. In the context of climate change, data analytics helps process massive datasets from sources such as sensors, satellites, and historical records. This enables better monitoring of environmental conditions, identification of trends, and evaluation of policy effectiveness.

Together, ML, deep learning, and data analytics form the core of most AI applications for climate change. By learning from vast and diverse datasets, these tools make it possible to anticipate risks, optimize resource use, and respond quickly to new information—enhancing the ability of communities, organizations, and policymakers to tackle the evolving challenges of a changing climate.

2.2 Data Requirements and Climate Data Sources

AI systems depend heavily on the availability and quality of data to function effectively, especially when applied to climate change adaptation and mitigation. For AI models to deliver accurate predictions, reliable insights, and actionable recommendations, they require large volumes of diverse, timely, and representative data covering environmental, climatic, and socioeconomic variables.

Key data requirements for climate-focused AI applications include high-resolution spatial and temporal data. This means collecting information that is geographically precise and updated frequently enough to capture changing conditions. For example, effective monitoring of weather events or deforestation relies on datasets that track changes at the local, regional, and global scales in near real time. Consistency, accuracy, and completeness are also essential—gaps or errors in data can significantly undermine the reliability of AI outputs.

There are multiple sources of climate and environmental data. Satellite imagery, provided by agencies such as NASA, the European Space Agency, and national meteorological organizations, is a major source of global data on land cover, sea surface temperatures, atmospheric composition, and more. Remote sensing technologies—using sensors mounted on satellites, aircraft, or drones—supply high-resolution information on everything from vegetation health to glacier movement.

Ground-based monitoring networks also play a vital role. These include weather stations, river gauges, air quality sensors, and soil moisture probes, which supply continuous streams of localized data. In addition, the IoT is expanding the reach of data collection, with networks of smart sensors gathering detailed measurements from urban infrastructure, agricultural fields, and industrial sites.

Historical climate records and reanalysis datasets are used to build long-term models, understand trends, and assess the impacts of interventions. Open data platforms, such as the World Bank Climate Data Portal and Copernicus Climate Data Store, offer valuable repositories for researchers and policymakers seeking to harness data for AI-driven solutions.

Despite these advances, data gaps remain, particularly in low-resource settings or regions with limited monitoring infrastructure. Addressing issues of accessibility, standardization, and interoperability is critical for realizing the full potential of AI in climate action. Ensuring data is shared, reliable, and used responsibly supports the creation of effective, equitable, and transparent AI systems that can help societies adapt to and mitigate the impacts of climate change.

2.3 Modeling Uncertainty and Risk with AI

Climate change is marked by significant complexity and uncertainty, making it challenging to forecast future conditions and assess risks accurately. AI offers advanced methods to address these challenges by modeling uncertainty and supporting better risk management. AI systems excel at analyzing vast datasets, identifying subtle patterns, and making probabilistic predictions, all of which are vital for understanding and responding to climate-related risks.

One of the strengths of AI, particularly ML, is its ability to incorporate a range of variables and account for interactions that traditional models may overlook. By using historical data alongside real-time inputs, AI models can generate forecasts that include confidence intervals or probability distributions, rather than single-point estimates. This probabilistic approach allows decision-makers to understand the range of possible outcomes and the likelihood of various scenarios, supporting more robust planning and resource allocation.

AI is also valuable in scenario analysis, which is essential for climate adaptation and mitigation. ML algorithms can simulate how changes in key drivers—such as greenhouse gas emissions, land use, or policy interventions—affect future climate conditions. These models help identify vulnerabilities, prioritize areas for intervention, and estimate the costs and benefits of different strategies under uncertainty.

Uncertainty is inherent not only in future climate projections but also in the data itself. AI can be used to assess data quality, fill in gaps, and quantify the impact of missing or noisy data on model results. This capacity is particularly important in regions where climate monitoring networks are sparse or incomplete.

Risk assessment is another area where AI provides significant value. By integrating data from diverse sources—weather forecasts, infrastructure records, population data, and more—AI systems can help predict the likelihood and potential impacts of extreme events such as floods, droughts, and heatwaves. These insights enable communities, businesses, and governments to prepare more effectively, allocate resources efficiently, and design adaptive strategies that are flexible in the face of uncertainty.

Overall, AI's strengths in modeling uncertainty and risk provide critical support for climate decision-making. By embracing the probabilistic and data-driven capabilities of AI, society can better navigate the unpredictable and dynamic landscape of climate change.

2.4 Ethics and Responsible AI for Climate Action

As AI becomes more deeply embedded in climate change adaptation and mitigation strategies, ethical considerations and responsible development practices are increasingly important. AI's power to shape decisions, allocate resources, and influence policy brings both opportunities and risks, making it essential to prioritize fairness, transparency, and accountability in every stage of AI deployment.

A foundational ethical concern is the risk of bias in AI systems. If algorithms are trained on incomplete or unrepresentative data, they may produce results that disadvantage certain communities or reinforce existing inequalities. In the climate context, this could mean prioritizing solutions that benefit regions with better data coverage while neglecting vulnerable populations with limited monitoring infrastructure. To mitigate bias, developers must strive for diverse, high-quality data and continuously test systems for unintended impacts.

Transparency is another critical principle. The decision-making processes of AI systems—sometimes described as "black boxes"—can be difficult to interpret, particularly with complex models like deep neural networks. Clear documentation, open-source code, and explainable AI techniques help ensure that stakeholders can understand, trust, and validate the results. This is especially vital when AI is used to guide public policy, enforce regulations, or make decisions affecting people's livelihoods.

Data privacy and security are also essential. AI applications in climate action often involve large-scale data collection, including information about land use, infrastructure, or even individual behaviors. Protecting sensitive data from misuse or unauthorized access is necessary to maintain public trust and comply with legal standards.

Accountability must be built into the design and deployment of AI systems. This involves defining who is responsible for the outcomes of AI-driven decisions and establishing mechanisms for redress if harm occurs. Ethical frameworks, regulatory oversight, and community engagement are valuable tools to ensure that AI is used responsibly.

Finally, the benefits of AI for climate action should be accessible and equitable. Efforts must be made to close the digital divide and include voices from different regions, backgrounds, and sectors in the design and implementation of AI solutions.

By centering ethics and responsibility, AI can be harnessed as a force for good, supporting fair and effective climate action while minimizing risks and building trust among all stakeholders.

2.5 Principles for Effective AI Use in Climate Solutions

Effectively deploying AI in climate adaptation and mitigation requires adherence to a set of guiding principles that ensure both technical robustness and societal benefit. These principles help maximize the value of AI, reduce unintended consequences, and foster trust among users and stakeholders.

One key principle is data quality and relevance. AI models depend on large volumes of accurate, up-to-date, and representative data to deliver reliable insights. This means prioritizing the collection and integration of diverse datasets from multiple sources, including satellite imagery, sensor networks, and historical climate records. Addressing gaps and inconsistencies in data is essential to minimize errors and biases in AI-driven decisions.

Interdisciplinary collaboration is also fundamental. The challenges posed by climate change cross disciplinary boundaries, involving experts in environmental science, engineering, data science, policy, and more. Bringing together knowledge from these fields supports the development of AI tools that are scientifically sound, contextually appropriate, and practically useful. Engaging local communities and stakeholders further enhances the relevance and acceptance of AI solutions.

Transparency and explainability are critical for building trust and enabling informed decision-making. Clear documentation of data sources, modeling choices, and algorithm logic helps users understand how AI-driven recommendations are generated. Where possible, incorporating explainable AI techniques allows stakeholders to interrogate and validate results, increasing accountability and reducing the risk of unintended harm.

Scalability and adaptability are important considerations as well. Climate challenges can vary greatly by region, sector, and over time. AI systems should be designed to be flexible, capable of evolving as new data becomes available or as priorities shift. Open standards and modular design approaches help ensure that solutions can be adapted and scaled to different contexts.

Finally, equity and inclusion must be prioritized throughout the AI lifecycle. This includes ensuring that underrepresented regions and populations benefit from AI innovations and that the risks of exclusion or negative impacts are minimized. Proactive steps to bridge the digital divide, foster capacity building, and support responsible technology transfer are crucial.

By following these principles—focusing on data quality, fostering collaboration, ensuring transparency, supporting scalability, and promoting inclusion—AI can be a powerful and responsible tool in the global response to climate change, delivering real-world impact while safeguarding public trust.

2.6 Chapter Summary

This chapter provided an overview of the foundational concepts and practical considerations for using AI in climate change adaptation and mitigation. It began by outlining the key types of AI most relevant to climate action—ML, deep learning, and data analytics—and explained how each contributes unique capabilities to data analysis, forecasting, and decision-making. The discussion emphasized that leveraging these AI approaches effectively depends on the availability of high-quality, comprehensive, and timely data from a range of sources, including satellites, ground-based sensors, and historical records.

Attention was also given to the importance of modeling uncertainty and risk, a critical function of AI in the climate context. By generating probabilistic forecasts and scenario analyses, AI enables decision-makers to better understand potential outcomes and to plan for a range of possible futures, rather than relying solely on single-point predictions.

The chapter also explored ethical considerations and responsible AI use, highlighting issues such as bias, transparency, data privacy, and accountability. These concerns underscore the necessity of thoughtful governance and robust safeguards to ensure AI serves the public good and supports equitable climate solutions. Principles for effective AI deployment—ranging from data quality and interdisciplinary collaboration to transparency, scalability, and inclusion—were identified as essential for maximizing AI's impact and ensuring societal benefit.

By covering these topics, the chapter laid a strong foundation for the more detailed exploration of AI applications in energy, water, agriculture, urban planning, and policy that follows in subsequent chapters. It reinforced that while AI holds significant promise for climate adaptation and mitigation, its success relies on careful planning, inclusive practices, and a steadfast commitment to ethical standards.

Chapter 3: AI in Climate Change Mitigation—Energy Systems

Chapter 3 explores the transformative impact of AI on energy systems as a central pillar of climate change mitigation. As societies shift toward low-carbon economies, the integration of renewable energy sources, smart grids, and advanced efficiency measures has become increasingly important—and increasingly complex. AI offers powerful solutions to many of these challenges, enabling smarter forecasting, dynamic optimization, and predictive maintenance across energy infrastructure. This chapter examines how AI is used to forecast renewable generation, balance electricity supply and demand, reduce emissions, and improve the efficiency of both centralized and distributed energy systems. Key topics include the role of AI in integrating variable renewables, managing demand, monitoring emissions, and supporting market operations. Through these applications, AI not only accelerates the decarbonization of the energy sector but also enhances reliability, cost-effectiveness, and resilience in the face of a changing climate.

3.1 AI for Renewable Energy Integration

Integrating renewable energy sources like solar, wind, and hydropower into electricity grids is a cornerstone of climate change mitigation. However, the variability and unpredictability of these resources present significant challenges for grid stability and reliable power supply. AI offers powerful tools to address these challenges and accelerate the global transition to clean energy.

AI excels at analyzing large and complex datasets from weather forecasts, historical energy production, and real-time grid operations. By processing this information, AI algorithms can accurately predict renewable energy generation, such as forecasting how much solar or wind power will be available at a given time and location. These forecasts help grid operators balance supply and demand, reduce reliance on fossil fuel backup systems, and minimize energy curtailment—when renewable energy output exceeds what the grid can handle.

AI also enables real-time optimization of energy systems. Advanced control algorithms can automatically adjust the operation of power plants, batteries, and other grid assets to respond to fluctuations in renewable output and electricity demand. This dynamic management improves grid flexibility, maximizes the use of clean energy, and enhances system reliability. For example, AI can coordinate distributed energy resources, such as rooftop solar panels and electric vehicles, turning them into "virtual power plants" that collectively support grid stability.

Another important application is predictive maintenance. AI-driven systems analyze sensor data from wind turbines, solar panels, and other equipment to detect early signs of wear or failure. By predicting when maintenance is needed, these systems can reduce downtime, lower operational costs, and extend the lifespan of renewable energy assets.

AI can also support energy market optimization, helping utilities and independent power producers make better decisions about when and where to buy or sell electricity. By factoring in price trends, demand patterns, and renewable generation forecasts, AI improves market efficiency and supports the financial viability of renewable energy investments.

Overall, the integration of AI into renewable energy systems is essential for overcoming technical and operational barriers. By enabling smarter forecasting, dynamic optimization, predictive maintenance, and improved market participation, AI plays a key role in expanding the role of renewables in the global energy mix and driving progress toward a low-carbon future.

3.2 Smart Grids and Demand-Side Management

The shift toward cleaner energy systems requires a more flexible and intelligent electricity grid. Smart grids—electricity networks enhanced with digital communications and automation—are essential for integrating renewables and responding to rapidly changing energy needs. AI is at the heart of this transformation, enabling advanced demand-side management and real-time coordination across the grid.

Smart grids leverage AI to process data from millions of sensors, smart meters, and devices connected throughout the power system. This information includes real-time electricity usage, voltage and frequency measurements, weather data, and even household or business energy consumption patterns. AI algorithms use these inputs to monitor grid conditions, detect anomalies, and optimize the flow of electricity, making the grid more resilient and adaptive to fluctuations in both supply and demand.

A key benefit of AI in smart grids is demand-side management—the ability to influence or control electricity consumption at the user level. AI-powered systems can forecast when and where energy demand will peak, allowing utilities to offer incentives, automate device settings, or remotely manage appliances to reduce strain on the grid during busy periods. For example, AI can help coordinate when electric vehicles are charged, shift industrial processes to off-peak times, or adjust heating and cooling systems to balance load without compromising comfort or productivity.

By actively engaging consumers in energy management, smart grids supported by AI help flatten demand peaks and reduce the need for costly and polluting backup power plants. They also make it possible to accommodate a higher share of renewable energy, whose generation may not always align with traditional demand patterns. Additionally, AI-driven demand response programs can enhance grid reliability during extreme weather events or equipment failures by quickly reallocating or reducing demand where needed.

Cybersecurity and data privacy are important considerations as grids become smarter and more connected. AI can assist by identifying unusual activity and defending against cyber threats, but strong safeguards must be maintained to protect sensitive information.

Ultimately, the integration of AI into smart grids and demand-side management is a crucial step toward building a cleaner, more efficient, and more resilient energy system. By enabling real-time data analysis, predictive control, and active participation from users, AI helps modern grids meet the evolving challenges of the energy transition and climate change.

3.3 AI for Energy Forecasting and Optimization

Accurate forecasting and efficient optimization are fundamental to managing modern energy systems, especially as the share of variable renewable resources like wind and solar continues to grow. AI offers powerful methods for predicting energy demand, renewable generation, and system behavior, enabling better planning, smoother operations, and more sustainable outcomes.

AI-driven forecasting relies on advanced algorithms that analyze vast amounts of historical and real-time data, including weather patterns, market prices, energy consumption records, and grid performance indicators. ML models can identify subtle trends and correlations that traditional statistical approaches might miss. For example, by combining meteorological data with local sensor readings, AI can predict the output of a solar farm or wind park hours or even days in advance. This level of precision allows grid operators to make informed decisions about resource allocation, reserve capacity, and energy trading.

Optimization is another key area where AI excels. Energy systems are inherently complex, with countless variables influencing supply, demand, storage, and distribution. AI-powered optimization tools can balance these factors in real time, automatically adjusting the operation of generators, batteries, and flexible loads to maximize efficiency and minimize costs. For instance, AI can coordinate the charging and discharging of energy storage systems to store surplus renewable energy during periods of low demand and release it when demand peaks, reducing reliance on fossil fuels.

AI also enhances operational reliability by anticipating and mitigating potential problems. Predictive analytics can flag equipment that is likely to fail, suggest optimal maintenance schedules, and recommend system adjustments to prevent outages. In energy markets, AI supports real-time bidding and price optimization, helping utilities and producers respond swiftly to changing conditions and market signals.

Moreover, AI-driven solutions facilitate sector coupling—integrating electricity, heating, transportation, and industry—to make the overall energy system more flexible and responsive. By linking different sectors and optimizing their energy use, AI helps reduce emissions, lower costs, and support the broader transition to a low-carbon economy.

In summary, AI is a critical enabler of energy forecasting and optimization, providing the insights and automation needed to efficiently manage increasingly complex and dynamic energy systems. Its adoption accelerates the integration of renewables and advances progress toward sustainable and resilient energy futures.

3.4 Emission Monitoring and Reduction with AI

Monitoring and reducing greenhouse gas emissions are central to climate change mitigation, yet traditional approaches can be limited by the scale and complexity of modern energy systems and industrial activities. AI is transforming these efforts by enabling more precise, efficient, and real-time monitoring, as well as supporting targeted strategies for emission reduction.

AI-powered systems can process data from a wide variety of sources, including satellite imagery, remote sensors, industrial monitoring equipment, and open-access databases. By analyzing this continuous flow of information, AI algorithms can identify emission hotspots, detect leaks or irregularities in infrastructure, and estimate emissions with greater accuracy than manual methods. This is particularly valuable in sectors such as power generation, oil and gas, transportation, and manufacturing, where emissions can vary greatly by process, location, and operating conditions.

Advanced image analysis, for example, allows AI to detect methane leaks from pipelines or flares, track deforestation rates, and monitor land use changes—all of which have significant climate impacts. ML models can integrate weather data, facility records, and historical trends to refine emissions inventories and support regulatory compliance.

Beyond monitoring, AI also plays a crucial role in emission reduction. By optimizing the operation of equipment, adjusting process parameters in real time, and predicting when and where emissions are likely to spike, AI helps companies minimize waste and energy use. In the energy sector, AI can automatically balance power generation from different sources to prioritize renewables and reduce reliance on fossil fuels. In transportation, AI-driven route planning and logistics optimization cut fuel consumption and lower emissions from vehicle fleets.

AI-enabled systems support transparency and accountability by generating detailed, up-to-date emissions reports for regulators, investors, and the public. This improved visibility not only helps organizations meet reporting obligations but also drives continuous improvement by identifying the most cost-effective pathways to further emission reductions.

Importantly, AI's role in emission monitoring and reduction is not limited to large organizations; it is increasingly being integrated into urban management systems, small businesses, and even consumer devices. By scaling up and democratizing access to powerful analytics, AI is helping accelerate progress toward national and global climate targets, supporting a more sustainable and accountable future.

3.5 Enhancing Energy Efficiency via AI Controls

Improving energy efficiency is one of the fastest and most cost-effective ways to reduce greenhouse gas emissions and advance climate goals. AI is playing a pivotal role in this effort by enabling sophisticated control systems that optimize energy use in real time across buildings, industry, and infrastructure.

AI-based controls can analyze large volumes of data from sensors, meters, and other monitoring devices to identify patterns, predict demand, and adjust system operations for maximum efficiency. In commercial and residential buildings, AI algorithms manage heating, cooling, lighting, and appliance usage, responding dynamically to occupancy levels, weather conditions, and user preferences. For example, AI can automatically lower heating or cooling when rooms are unoccupied, adjust lighting based on natural daylight, or schedule energy-intensive tasks for off-peak hours, all without human intervention.

In industrial settings, AI-driven control systems optimize complex production processes by continuously monitoring variables such as temperature, pressure, and flow rates. ML models learn from historical and real-time operational data to identify inefficiencies, anticipate equipment needs, and make micro-adjustments that minimize energy waste. This not only cuts emissions but also reduces operating costs and extends the lifespan of machinery.

AI also contributes to efficiency at the system level, especially in integrated infrastructure such as district energy networks, water systems, and smart cities. By coordinating the operation of distributed assets—like combined heat and power plants, renewable energy sources, and battery storage—AI ensures that energy is produced and consumed in the most efficient manner possible. These systems can quickly adapt to changing demand, grid conditions, or external factors like weather and market prices.

Another key benefit of AI controls is predictive maintenance. By analyzing data on equipment performance, AI can forecast when maintenance is required, preventing energy losses due to malfunction or wear and reducing unplanned downtime.

Importantly, AI-enabled energy efficiency solutions are becoming more accessible and affordable, allowing small businesses, homeowners, and municipalities to benefit from advanced optimization tools. As more sectors adopt these intelligent controls, the collective impact on energy savings and emissions reductions grows, supporting a more sustainable, cost-effective, and climate-resilient energy future.

3.6 Chapter Summary

This chapter explored the transformative role of AI in modernizing energy systems and accelerating climate change mitigation. It began by examining how AI supports the integration of renewable energy sources into power grids, overcoming challenges related to variability and grid stability. AI's ability to forecast renewable generation and optimize system operations enables greater reliance on clean energy while maintaining reliability and efficiency.

The chapter then addressed the emergence of smart grids and the importance of demand-side management. AI-driven systems help utilities balance electricity supply and demand in real time, empower consumers to participate actively in energy management, and facilitate the integration of distributed resources. By enabling predictive and adaptive control, AI enhances grid flexibility, security, and resilience.

Attention was also given to AI's applications in energy forecasting and optimization. AI models analyze vast amounts of data to predict energy production, demand, and market dynamics with high precision. This supports efficient resource allocation, storage management, and market participation, all of which are critical for decarbonizing energy systems.

Emission monitoring and reduction were highlighted as another area where AI brings significant value. By automating data collection, analyzing diverse information sources, and optimizing operational practices, AI helps organizations track and lower greenhouse gas emissions more effectively. Enhanced energy efficiency, supported by AI-based controls, was discussed as a major pathway to reduce both emissions and costs across sectors.

In summary, AI is a powerful enabler of cleaner, smarter, and more sustainable energy systems. Its deployment across forecasting, optimization, emissions management, and efficiency improvement is accelerating the global shift toward a low-carbon future, providing vital support in the fight against climate change.

Chapter 4: AI for Decarbonizing Industry and Infrastructure

Chapter 4 delves into the essential role of AI in decarbonizing industry and infrastructure—two sectors that account for a significant share of global emissions and resource consumption. As pressure mounts for cleaner production and more efficient use of resources, AI is emerging as a critical tool for transforming how industries operate and how infrastructure is managed. This chapter examines how AI enables process optimization, predictive maintenance, and real-time monitoring within factories and supply chains, driving substantial gains in efficiency and emissions reduction. It also explores how AI supports the development of innovative materials, advances the circular economy, and improves the sustainability of large-scale infrastructure projects. By unlocking new pathways for operational excellence and resource stewardship, AI is helping industries and infrastructure providers meet ambitious climate targets while maintaining competitiveness and resilience in a rapidly evolving landscape.

4.1 Process Optimization in Manufacturing

Manufacturing is a resource-intensive sector that significantly contributes to greenhouse gas emissions, energy consumption, and environmental impact. Optimizing processes within manufacturing is therefore essential for both improving efficiency and advancing climate change mitigation. AI is increasingly being used to achieve these goals by enabling data-driven decision-making, real-time monitoring, and advanced automation.

AI-powered process optimization begins with the collection and analysis of vast datasets from sensors embedded throughout the manufacturing facility. These sensors monitor variables such as temperature, pressure, material flow, equipment performance, and energy usage. ML algorithms process this information to identify patterns, inefficiencies, and potential improvements. By continuously analyzing data from ongoing operations, AI systems can suggest adjustments to production schedules, resource allocation, and machinery settings that minimize waste and reduce energy consumption.

Predictive analytics play a critical role in anticipating problems before they occur. AI can identify subtle signs of wear or malfunction in equipment, enabling predictive maintenance and reducing the risk of costly breakdowns and production delays. This not only improves operational efficiency but also prolongs the lifespan of machinery, further lowering resource use and emissions.

Another advantage of AI-driven optimization is adaptive control. As conditions change—such as fluctuations in raw material quality, varying demand, or shifts in energy prices—AI systems can dynamically adjust processes to maintain optimal performance. This adaptability is especially valuable in sectors that experience frequent disruptions or require precise quality control.

AI also supports waste reduction by analyzing material flows and production outcomes. Algorithms can detect sources of excess scrap, emissions, or defects, enabling targeted interventions to streamline resource use and improve product quality. Over time, these incremental improvements lead to significant reductions in both environmental impact and operational costs.

The integration of AI in manufacturing extends beyond the individual factory. Networked AI systems can coordinate supply chains, synchronize production across multiple facilities, and support broader sustainability goals. By leveraging real-time data and advanced analytics, manufacturers are better equipped to balance productivity, profitability, and environmental responsibility, making process optimization a cornerstone of sustainable industry in the era of climate change.

4.2 Monitoring and Reducing Supply Chain Emissions

Supply chains are often vast and complex, stretching across multiple regions and involving a diverse range of suppliers, transportation networks, and production processes. These interconnected activities can account for a significant portion of a company's total greenhouse gas emissions, making effective monitoring and reduction essential for climate change mitigation. AI is rapidly transforming the way organizations manage supply chain emissions by providing the tools needed for comprehensive tracking, analysis, and intervention.

AI enables more granular and accurate emissions monitoring throughout the entire supply chain. By integrating data from a variety of sources—such as supplier records, shipment tracking, sensor networks, and external databases—AI systems build a detailed picture of emissions at every stage, from raw material extraction to product delivery. ML algorithms process this information to identify emission hotspots, inefficiencies, and high-impact intervention points that might be missed through manual methods or traditional reporting.

With these insights, companies can prioritize actions that yield the greatest emissions reductions. AI can recommend alternative suppliers with lower carbon footprints, optimize transportation routes to minimize fuel consumption, and propose changes in packaging or manufacturing techniques to reduce waste. For example, algorithms can analyze shipment data in real time to identify opportunities for load consolidation or route adjustments, cutting unnecessary travel and associated emissions.

AI also plays a role in scenario modeling and forecasting, allowing organizations to evaluate the impact of different strategies before implementation. This helps companies balance emissions reduction goals with other operational objectives such as cost, speed, and reliability. By simulating various supply chain configurations, AI supports better decision-making and more sustainable planning.

Transparency and accountability are enhanced as well. AI-driven platforms can automate emissions reporting, generate real-time dashboards for managers and stakeholders, and ensure compliance with environmental regulations and voluntary sustainability standards. This level of visibility is increasingly important for meeting investor, consumer, and regulatory expectations regarding climate action.

Ultimately, leveraging AI for supply chain emissions management supports not only corporate sustainability targets but also broader climate goals. By providing accurate monitoring, actionable insights, and data-driven recommendations, AI empowers organizations to build more resilient, efficient, and low-carbon supply chains, helping to drive systemic change across industries.

4.3 Predictive Maintenance and Resource Efficiency

Predictive maintenance uses AI to monitor equipment and infrastructure in real time, identifying potential failures before they result in costly downtime or excessive resource use. In manufacturing and other industrial sectors, unplanned breakdowns can disrupt production, waste energy, and lead to unnecessary material consumption. AI-driven predictive maintenance addresses these challenges by collecting and analyzing data from sensors embedded in machinery, such as temperature, vibration, pressure, and operational cycles.

ML algorithms process this continuous flow of sensor data to recognize patterns associated with normal operation and those signaling wear or malfunction. As soon as early warning signs appear, the system can notify operators or trigger automatic adjustments, allowing maintenance teams to address issues proactively rather than reactively. This approach reduces unplanned outages, improves workplace safety, and helps companies allocate resources more efficiently by scheduling repairs only when they are truly needed.

Resource efficiency is further enhanced by minimizing the replacement of parts and avoiding excessive preventive maintenance, both of which can waste materials and increase emissions. AI-supported systems optimize spare parts inventory, track the health and lifespan of critical components, and provide insights on how operational adjustments can extend equipment life. When machines are maintained at optimal performance, energy consumption is lowered, emissions decrease, and production becomes more reliable.

The integration of predictive maintenance with broader resource management platforms enables real-time visibility across entire facilities or networks. Operators can monitor multiple assets simultaneously, prioritize maintenance activities based on risk and criticality, and coordinate interventions to minimize production interruptions. In addition, historical maintenance and operational data can be used to refine ML models over time, making them more accurate and responsive to changing conditions.

The application of predictive maintenance and resource efficiency is not limited to large factories or heavy industry. Utilities, transportation systems, commercial buildings, and even agricultural operations can benefit from these AI-driven solutions. As organizations continue to digitize their operations and deploy connected sensors, predictive maintenance is becoming a standard practice, supporting lower costs, reduced environmental impact, and more sustainable business models across sectors.

4.4 AI-driven Material Innovation

Material innovation plays a crucial role in addressing climate change by enabling the development of products and processes that are more sustainable, durable, and efficient. AI is accelerating progress in this area by transforming how new materials are discovered, tested, and deployed in manufacturing and other industries.

Traditional material discovery and optimization often involve lengthy trial-and-error experimentation. Researchers must sift through countless combinations of elements and compounds to identify those with desirable properties, a process that can take years.

AI streamlines this process by rapidly analyzing vast datasets of material structures, properties, and performance outcomes. ML algorithms can predict which combinations are most likely to exhibit target characteristics, significantly reducing the time and resources needed for laboratory experiments.

AI-driven simulations and modeling are essential tools for understanding how materials behave under different conditions. These models can assess factors such as strength, conductivity, thermal resistance, and recyclability without the need for physical prototypes. By virtually testing thousands of possibilities, researchers can focus their experimental efforts on the most promising candidates, accelerating the development of new materials for use in construction, transportation, electronics, and energy systems.

Material innovation supported by AI is advancing the creation of alternatives to high-emission or non-renewable materials. Examples include lightweight composites that reduce energy use in vehicles, advanced polymers for efficient solar panels, and new forms of insulation that improve energy efficiency in buildings. AI can also assist in designing materials that are easier to recycle or that use less harmful substances, supporting circular economy objectives.

Integration of AI into the materials supply chain provides additional sustainability benefits. Algorithms optimize sourcing, track material footprints, and suggest alternatives with lower environmental impacts. Manufacturers can use AI insights to select materials that not only meet performance requirements but also align with climate and sustainability targets.

As the need for climate-friendly solutions grows, AI-driven material innovation is reshaping how industries approach product design and resource use. The combination of advanced computation, big data, and domain expertise unlocks new possibilities for sustainable development and accelerates the transition to low-carbon, high-performance materials across sectors.

4.5 Enabling Circular Economy with AI

The circular economy model seeks to minimize waste, extend product lifecycles, and maximize the value of resources through reuse, recycling, and responsible management. Moving away from the traditional "take-make-dispose" approach requires new tools and strategies, and AI is emerging as a key enabler in making circular practices viable and scalable across industries.

AI systems help track products and materials throughout their lifecycle, from production and distribution to use, reuse, and end-of-life processing. By analyzing data from sensors, supply chains, and recycling facilities, AI can identify opportunities for resource recovery and suggest ways to redesign products for greater durability and easier disassembly. This visibility supports manufacturers in designing products that are easier to recycle, repair, or refurbish, reducing overall material waste.

In waste management and recycling operations, AI-driven technologies improve sorting efficiency and accuracy. Machine vision systems powered by AI can distinguish between different types of materials—such as plastics, metals, and paper—at high speed and with minimal human intervention. This enables more effective separation and processing, resulting in higher quality recycled materials and reduced contamination rates.

AI can also support predictive modeling for product usage and end-of-life management. By forecasting when products are likely to reach the end of their useful life, businesses can plan collection, refurbishment, or recycling efforts more efficiently. These insights enable more reliable supply chains for secondary materials and help shift industries toward closed-loop systems where waste becomes a valuable input for new products.

Additionally, AI-driven platforms facilitate the creation of digital marketplaces for sharing, trading, and reselling goods and materials.

This promotes product reuse and extends the lifespan of assets, further reducing demand for virgin resources.

The adoption of AI in enabling the circular economy also has important implications for sustainability reporting and compliance. Automated data collection and analysis provide transparency for consumers, regulators, and investors, helping to demonstrate progress toward sustainability goals and circularity commitments.

As organizations seek to reduce their environmental impact and build resilience in the face of resource constraints, integrating AI into circular economy strategies opens new pathways for innovation and efficiency. Through smarter design, improved material recovery, and better management of resource flows, AI is helping to redefine production and consumption for a more sustainable future.

4.6 Chapter Summary

This chapter examined the integration of AI into industrial and manufacturing processes as a pathway toward decarbonization and resource efficiency. The discussion began with how AI-driven process optimization enables manufacturers to monitor and fine-tune operations in real time, reducing waste, energy consumption, and emissions while maintaining productivity and quality standards.

Attention was given to the use of AI for monitoring and reducing emissions throughout complex supply chains. By providing detailed and timely insights across every stage of production and distribution, AI empowers organizations to identify emission hotspots, make more sustainable sourcing decisions, and achieve transparency for stakeholders and regulators.

The chapter also highlighted the role of predictive maintenance in increasing operational reliability and resource efficiency. AI systems that monitor equipment health and predict failures help minimize unplanned downtime, reduce material waste, and extend the useful life of machinery—all contributing to lower emissions and improved sustainability outcomes.

AI's contributions to material innovation were explored, emphasizing how ML and advanced modeling accelerate the discovery and optimization of new materials with reduced environmental footprints. These advances make it possible to replace high-emission materials and design products that are more sustainable from the outset.

The application of AI to enable circular economy practices was also addressed. By tracking materials, optimizing recycling, and forecasting end-of-life scenarios, AI supports more efficient resource use and helps close material loops in production systems.

Overall, this chapter illustrated that AI is transforming industrial and manufacturing sectors, driving both climate mitigation and competitive advantage. Through smarter process control, emissions monitoring, maintenance, material development, and circular strategies, AI is helping industries become more resilient, efficient, and aligned with global sustainability goals.

Chapter 5: AI in Climate Adaptation— Water Resources and Management

Chapter 5 focuses on the growing significance of AI in climate adaptation through smarter water resource management. As climate change intensifies water scarcity, variability, and extreme events such as droughts and floods, the ability to monitor, predict, and respond to water challenges is more critical than ever. AI technologies are enabling breakthroughs in forecasting weather and droughts, optimizing water distribution, modeling flood risks, and protecting water quality and ecosystem health. This chapter explores how AI-driven tools help utilities, governments, and communities manage water more efficiently, strengthen early warning systems, and adapt to new climate realities. With the capacity to analyze complex data from multiple sources and automate rapid response, AI is transforming water management practices to better safeguard people, economies, and ecosystems against climate risks.

5.1 Weather Forecasting, Drought Prediction, and Early Warning

Weather forecasting and early warning systems are essential components of climate adaptation, helping communities prepare for and respond to extreme events. Traditional forecasting methods rely on mathematical models and historical data, but AI is enhancing the accuracy, speed, and reliability of these systems by integrating vast datasets and identifying complex patterns that might otherwise go unnoticed.

AI algorithms process information from satellites, radar networks, weather stations, and remote sensors to produce more precise and localized forecasts. ML models can learn from historical weather patterns, current atmospheric conditions, and environmental variables to predict temperature, precipitation, wind, and other parameters with greater accuracy than conventional approaches. This capability is especially valuable for regions with highly variable weather or limited access to advanced meteorological infrastructure.

Drought prediction is another area where AI is making a significant impact. By analyzing data on soil moisture, rainfall, evaporation rates, vegetation health, and even socioeconomic factors, AI models can forecast the onset, severity, and duration of droughts. Early and accurate prediction enables governments, farmers, and water managers to implement timely interventions, such as adjusting water allocations, planning crop cycles, or activating emergency response plans. This reduces the risks associated with water scarcity and helps minimize economic and environmental losses.

Early warning systems benefit from AI's ability to detect anomalies and trigger alerts quickly. For example, AI can identify patterns that indicate the likelihood of flash floods, heatwaves, or severe storms before they happen. Automated systems can then disseminate warnings through multiple channels, reaching at-risk populations and authorities with enough lead time to take protective measures.

AI also contributes to the continuous improvement of forecasting and warning systems by learning from past events and updating models based on outcomes. This adaptive capability increases the resilience of communities and institutions to the impacts of climate change.

By strengthening weather forecasting, drought prediction, and early warning, AI provides a critical foundation for proactive climate adaptation, supporting faster, better-informed decisions and reducing the vulnerability of people and ecosystems to extreme weather and climate variability.

5.2 Optimizing Water Distribution and Usage

Efficient water distribution and usage are fundamental to building resilience against climate change, especially in regions facing increasing water stress and variability. AI is transforming how utilities, cities, and agricultural systems manage water resources, providing tools to optimize supply networks, reduce losses, and ensure that water is used where it is needed most.

AI systems can analyze vast amounts of real-time data from sensors embedded in water infrastructure, such as pipelines, reservoirs, and treatment plants. By continuously monitoring flow rates, pressure, and water quality, ML algorithms can detect leaks, identify inefficiencies, and forecast demand patterns. Early detection of leaks and anomalies enables rapid response, reducing water loss and the costs associated with unaccounted-for water. This approach not only conserves water but also saves energy and lowers operational expenses.

In urban settings, AI-driven platforms help manage complex distribution networks by balancing supply and demand across multiple neighborhoods, commercial centers, and industrial zones. Algorithms can predict periods of peak demand, optimize pumping schedules, and adjust operations based on changing weather, usage trends, and maintenance requirements. This dynamic management ensures that water delivery is reliable and efficient, even as conditions fluctuate.

Agricultural water use also benefits from AI optimization. ML models can analyze weather forecasts, soil moisture levels, crop types, and growth stages to recommend precise irrigation schedules tailored to the needs of individual fields. By providing farmers with actionable insights, AI reduces overwatering and runoff, conserves limited resources, and increases yields—making agriculture more resilient to droughts and other climate risks.

Water utilities are also using AI to plan long-term investments and manage assets more strategically. Predictive analytics inform decisions on infrastructure upgrades, expansion, and maintenance, helping to prioritize projects that will deliver the greatest benefits for reliability and sustainability.

By making water distribution and usage more efficient, AI helps communities and industries adapt to climate pressures, maintain economic stability, and protect vital ecosystems. These advancements are essential for addressing the increasing challenges of water scarcity, supporting climate adaptation efforts, and ensuring sustainable water management for future generations.

5.3 Flood Modeling and Risk Assessment

Floods are among the most damaging natural disasters, causing widespread loss of life, property damage, and disruption to communities. With climate change driving more intense rainfall events and altering hydrological cycles, the need for accurate flood modeling and effective risk assessment has become even more critical. AI is now at the forefront of efforts to predict, model, and manage flood risks with greater precision and timeliness.

AI-driven flood modeling combines data from a range of sources, including satellite imagery, ground-based sensors, weather forecasts, and historical flood records. ML algorithms process this information to simulate river flows, surface runoff, and floodplain dynamics under a variety of conditions. These models can account for changes in land use, urbanization, and climate variables, providing a detailed and dynamic understanding of flood risks across different scales and locations.

One of the major strengths of AI in this context is its ability to handle complex and nonlinear relationships between multiple variables. Traditional models may struggle to incorporate the vast and diverse data required for accurate flood prediction, but AI systems can learn from patterns in past events and apply this knowledge to forecast the likelihood, extent, and severity of future floods. Real-time data feeds enable AI to update forecasts rapidly as new information becomes available, supporting adaptive and responsive risk management.

AI is also transforming flood risk assessment for infrastructure and communities. By integrating data on population density, building types, critical facilities, and evacuation routes, AI tools can identify vulnerable areas and prioritize resources for flood prevention and response. Decision-makers gain insights into the effectiveness of proposed flood control measures—such as levees, reservoirs, and green infrastructure—before making costly investments.

Automated early warning systems powered by AI can detect unusual conditions and trigger timely alerts to authorities and the public, enabling faster evacuation and emergency response. These technologies reduce human error, improve situational awareness, and ultimately save lives.

The application of AI in flood modeling and risk assessment is enhancing society's ability to anticipate and manage flood risks in a changing climate. By providing more accurate, timely, and actionable insights, AI supports the development of safer, more resilient communities and helps protect lives and property from the increasing threats posed by extreme weather events.

5.4 Monitoring Water Quality and Ecosystem Health

Monitoring water quality and ecosystem health is vital for sustaining life, supporting economic activity, and ensuring environmental resilience in the face of climate change. Traditional water monitoring methods, while valuable, are often limited by the frequency and coverage of sampling, high costs, and time-consuming laboratory analysis. AI is transforming this field by enabling continuous, real-time assessment of water bodies and ecosystems at multiple scales.

AI-driven monitoring systems leverage data from a wide variety of sources, including in-situ sensors, remote sensing satellites, drones, and automated sampling devices. These technologies collect high-resolution data on water temperature, turbidity, dissolved oxygen, nutrient levels, and the presence of contaminants or toxins. ML algorithms process this vast stream of information to detect patterns, identify anomalies, and flag early signs of pollution, algal blooms, or ecosystem stress.

One important advantage of AI is its capacity to integrate and analyze heterogeneous datasets. AI models can combine physical, chemical, and biological data with information on land use, weather, and hydrological conditions, building a comprehensive picture of ecosystem health. This holistic approach helps researchers and water managers understand the causes of observed changes, predict future trends, and assess the impacts of interventions.

Real-time monitoring enabled by AI allows for rapid response to emerging threats. For example, if an AI system detects a sudden drop in dissolved oxygen or an increase in harmful bacteria, it can trigger automated alerts to relevant agencies or operators. This facilitates timely action to contain pollution, adjust treatment processes, or warn affected communities, reducing risks to human health and biodiversity.

AI is also improving the efficiency of long-term ecosystem management. Predictive analytics support planning for habitat restoration, invasive species control, and the maintenance of critical ecosystem services such as water purification and flood regulation. As climate change continues to pressure aquatic environments, these capabilities are essential for adaptive management and conservation.

By delivering detailed, timely, and actionable insights, AI strengthens efforts to safeguard water quality and ecosystem health. This not only supports climate adaptation and environmental protection but also ensures that vital water resources remain available for generations to come.

5.5 Managing Scarcity and Extreme Events with AI

Climate change is intensifying water scarcity and the frequency of extreme events such as droughts, floods, and heatwaves. Managing these challenges requires advanced tools that can predict, respond to, and minimize the impacts on communities and ecosystems. AI is playing an increasingly important role in equipping decision-makers with the insights and flexibility needed to navigate periods of scarcity and respond to extreme events.

AI systems can process large volumes of data from diverse sources, including weather forecasts, hydrological models, soil moisture sensors, and socioeconomic indicators. By integrating these datasets, ML models can assess vulnerability, predict the likelihood of water shortages, and estimate the potential consequences for agriculture, industry, and households. This holistic perspective enables authorities to implement targeted water conservation measures, optimize allocations, and prioritize interventions for those most at risk.

During extreme events such as droughts or floods, AI enables real-time monitoring and adaptive management. Algorithms track changes in water levels, flow rates, precipitation, and usage patterns, adjusting recommendations as conditions evolve. This helps water utilities and emergency managers make informed decisions about reservoir releases, groundwater pumping, and infrastructure operation, ensuring supplies are maintained and risks are minimized.

AI-driven early warning systems are critical for reducing the impacts of sudden or severe events. By identifying warning signs in environmental data—such as rapidly falling river levels or rising temperatures—AI can trigger timely alerts to authorities, farmers, and the public. These systems support proactive responses, such as activating contingency plans, reallocating resources, or issuing water use restrictions before conditions become critical.

In the longer term, AI supports scenario analysis and resilience planning by simulating the effects of different management strategies under various climate futures. This empowers planners to design more robust water systems, invest in adaptive infrastructure, and promote behaviors that conserve water and reduce vulnerability.

Through data integration, predictive modeling, and rapid response capabilities, AI is becoming an indispensable asset for managing water scarcity and extreme events. These innovations strengthen community resilience, safeguard livelihoods, and support sustainable adaptation as climate pressures continue to grow.

5.6 Chapter Summary

This chapter explored how AI is reshaping water resource management and adaptation to climate challenges. It began with the application of AI to weather forecasting, drought prediction, and early warning systems, highlighting how ML enhances the accuracy, speed, and localization of forecasts. These improvements provide communities with critical lead time to prepare for and mitigate the impacts of extreme weather events.

The chapter then addressed the optimization of water distribution and usage. AI systems are enabling utilities, cities, and agricultural sectors to monitor networks in real time, detect leaks, forecast demand, and deliver water more efficiently. These innovations help reduce losses, conserve resources, and build resilience in regions facing growing water stress.

Flood modeling and risk assessment were discussed as vital areas where AI processes complex and dynamic data to improve predictions and inform infrastructure and emergency planning. AI's ability to rapidly integrate multiple variables supports better management of flood risks and helps protect vulnerable populations and assets.

The use of AI in monitoring water quality and ecosystem health was also emphasized. Continuous, real-time analysis of diverse data streams allows for early detection of pollution and environmental stress, enabling faster responses and better long-term management of aquatic systems.

Finally, the chapter examined how AI supports the management of water scarcity and extreme events by providing holistic assessments, real-time adaptation, and early warnings. AI-driven scenario analysis and resilience planning help ensure that water systems and communities can adapt to a wide range of future challenges.

Across all these domains, AI is proving indispensable in building adaptive capacity and supporting sustainable water management under climate change. By delivering actionable insights, improving efficiency, and enhancing preparedness, AI is helping societies safeguard water resources for present and future generations.

Chapter 6: AI for Sustainable Agriculture and Land Use

Chapter 6 explores the pivotal role of AI in advancing sustainable agriculture and land use amid a changing climate. As pressures on food production systems and natural landscapes intensify, AI is offering innovative solutions to enhance resilience, efficiency, and sustainability. This chapter examines how AI-powered tools are transforming precision agriculture—enabling targeted crop, pest, and yield management—as well as supporting soil health assessment, land use change monitoring, and biodiversity conservation. It also addresses the application of AI in building more resilient food systems and promoting adaptive land management practices. By integrating diverse data sources and generating actionable insights, AI empowers farmers, land managers, and policymakers to optimize resource use, reduce environmental impact, and adapt to evolving climate challenges. Through these advancements, AI is helping to secure food supplies and protect critical ecosystems for future generations.

6.1 Precision Agriculture: Crop, Pest, and Yield Management

Precision agriculture is revolutionizing how farmers manage crops, pests, and yields by integrating AI into decision-making processes. Traditional farming methods often rely on uniform applications of water, fertilizer, and pesticides across entire fields, leading to inefficiencies, wasted resources, and environmental harm. AI-powered precision agriculture allows for targeted, data-driven interventions that optimize inputs, boost productivity, and minimize negative impacts.

ML models analyze data from a variety of sources, including soil sensors, satellite imagery, drones, weather forecasts, and historical yield records. This information provides a detailed understanding of field conditions, crop health, and pest activity at a much finer scale than previously possible. By identifying patterns and trends, AI algorithms can recommend precise actions—such as variable-rate irrigation, fertilizer application, or targeted pest control—that deliver resources exactly where and when they are needed.

AI-based pest management tools help detect and predict outbreaks of harmful insects, diseases, or weeds. By continuously monitoring environmental conditions and plant health indicators, these systems alert farmers to emerging threats, allowing for timely and efficient interventions. This reduces the need for broad-spectrum pesticide applications, protecting beneficial species and lowering chemical use.

Yield management is another area where AI delivers value. Predictive models integrate data on planting dates, soil properties, weather patterns, and crop growth stages to estimate likely yields and identify potential bottlenecks. Farmers can use these forecasts to make informed decisions about harvest timing, resource allocation, and market strategies.

The benefits of AI-driven precision agriculture extend beyond increased productivity and profitability. By reducing excessive use of water, fertilizer, and chemicals, precision agriculture lowers input costs, conserves natural resources, and lessens environmental impact. This is particularly important as climate change introduces greater uncertainty and variability into farming systems.

With continued advances in sensors, connectivity, and data analytics, AI-enabled precision agriculture is becoming increasingly accessible to farms of all sizes. These innovations are equipping farmers to meet the challenges of a changing climate, support food security, and manage land in a more sustainable and resilient manner.

6.2 Soil Health Assessment and Management

Healthy soils are fundamental to sustainable agriculture, food security, and ecosystem resilience, yet they are increasingly threatened by climate change, intensive land use, and pollution. AI is providing new ways to assess and manage soil health, enabling farmers and land managers to monitor conditions in real time, predict potential problems, and implement practices that preserve or restore soil quality.

AI systems can analyze large and diverse datasets from soil sensors, remote sensing imagery, weather records, and laboratory analyses. These data streams provide insights into critical soil properties such as moisture content, organic matter, nutrient levels, pH, compaction, and microbial activity. By applying ML algorithms, AI can identify patterns and relationships that might be missed by traditional analysis, offering a more complete understanding of soil health across different fields and landscapes.

Through the integration of real-time and historical data, AI models can detect early signs of soil degradation, such as declining fertility, increasing salinity, or erosion risks. These tools can forecast how soil conditions will change under different management scenarios or weather patterns, helping farmers make informed decisions about crop rotations, cover cropping, tillage practices, and nutrient application. This proactive approach supports the adoption of regenerative practices that build soil resilience and productivity over the long term.

AI-driven recommendations can be tailored to the specific needs of individual plots or zones within a farm, rather than applying a one-size-fits-all approach. This precision reduces input costs and minimizes negative environmental impacts, such as nutrient runoff or soil carbon loss. Farmers benefit from more efficient use of fertilizers and amendments, improved crop yields, and healthier soil ecosystems.

Monitoring and managing soil health with AI also supports broader sustainability goals. Healthy soils store more carbon, regulate water flow, and provide habitat for biodiversity, all of which are critical for climate change adaptation and mitigation. By equipping farmers with actionable insights and adaptive strategies, AI is helping to ensure that soils remain a resilient foundation for agriculture and the environment in a changing world.

6.3 Land Use Change Monitoring and Prevention

Land use change—such as deforestation, urban sprawl, and the conversion of natural habitats to agricultural or industrial uses—has profound effects on climate, biodiversity, and ecosystem services. As these pressures intensify with global development and population growth, AI is becoming an essential tool for monitoring and preventing unsustainable land use change.

AI-powered monitoring systems integrate data from satellites, aerial drones, remote sensors, and geospatial databases to provide near real-time assessments of land cover and land use patterns. ML algorithms process vast quantities of imagery and spatial data to detect subtle changes in vegetation, soil, and surface features. These systems can distinguish between natural shifts—such as seasonal changes—and human-driven activities like illegal logging, land clearing, or unauthorized construction.

One of the major advantages of AI in this context is its ability to continuously analyze large geographic areas and identify early warning signs of land use change. Automated alerts can notify authorities or land managers about potential deforestation events, habitat loss, or encroachment, enabling faster and more effective responses. This early detection is vital for enforcing land protection policies and supporting conservation efforts.

AI also aids in prevention by supporting predictive modeling and scenario analysis. By combining land use data with information on economic drivers, population trends, and infrastructure development, AI can forecast where land use pressures are likely to emerge. Policymakers and planners can use these insights to guide zoning, prioritize conservation areas, and design interventions that balance development needs with environmental protection.

Data-driven land use planning, supported by AI, helps minimize conflicts over resources and supports the sustainable allocation of land for agriculture, urban development, and conservation. These systems can also evaluate the effectiveness of existing land management strategies, highlighting where adjustments are needed to achieve climate and biodiversity targets.

Empowering communities and decision-makers with timely, accurate information is key to addressing land use challenges. As AI technologies become more accessible and user-friendly, they are expanding the capacity of organizations and governments to safeguard critical landscapes and prevent irreversible environmental damage. By improving monitoring and supporting proactive management, AI is playing a vital role in promoting more sustainable and resilient land use practices.

6.4 Deforestation Detection and Biodiversity Conservation

Deforestation remains one of the leading drivers of biodiversity loss, greenhouse gas emissions, and ecosystem degradation worldwide. Monitoring and preventing deforestation, as well as supporting broader biodiversity conservation goals, require timely and accurate information about land cover changes and the health of natural habitats. AI is transforming these efforts by automating the detection of deforestation and enabling more effective conservation strategies.

AI-powered systems use data from satellites, aerial imagery, drones, and ground-based sensors to monitor forests and other natural areas over large regions and long time frames. ML algorithms are trained to recognize patterns associated with tree loss, fragmentation, or degradation. These models can distinguish between natural disturbances, such as wildfires or storms, and human activities like logging, land clearing, or road construction. By analyzing changes in vegetation cover, canopy structure, and surface reflectance, AI provides near real-time alerts of deforestation events, enabling authorities and conservation groups to respond quickly and target enforcement actions where they are most needed.

Beyond detection, AI supports biodiversity conservation by mapping habitats, identifying key species, and monitoring ecosystem health. Algorithms can process vast and complex datasets to track animal populations, migration patterns, and changes in plant communities. These insights help prioritize areas for protection, guide restoration projects, and assess the effectiveness of conservation interventions over time.

Predictive modeling is another area where AI delivers value. By integrating information on climate trends, land use pressures, and species distributions, AI can forecast future risks to habitats and biodiversity. Planners and policymakers use these forecasts to design adaptive management strategies that enhance ecosystem resilience and support long-term conservation goals.

Community engagement also benefits from AI-driven tools, such as smartphone apps and online platforms, which allow citizen scientists to contribute data on wildlife sightings, habitat conditions, or illegal activities. These participatory approaches expand the reach of monitoring networks and foster broader support for conservation.

As deforestation and biodiversity loss remain critical global challenges, AI is providing the intelligence, scale, and speed needed to protect natural ecosystems. Through automated detection, advanced modeling, and inclusive data collection, AI is strengthening efforts to conserve biodiversity and sustain the vital services that healthy forests and habitats provide.

6.5 AI-Powered Food System Resilience

Building resilience in food systems is essential to ensure food security and nutritional health in the face of climate change, population growth, and evolving economic pressures. AI is playing a pivotal role in enhancing the adaptability and robustness of food systems, supporting actors from farm to fork with timely, data-driven insights.

AI can analyze large, complex datasets that encompass crop performance, weather forecasts, market trends, supply chain dynamics, and consumer demand. By integrating these sources, AI-powered platforms provide farmers, food processors, distributors, and retailers with actionable intelligence for planning, resource allocation, and risk management. For example, ML models can help anticipate harvest shortfalls, shifts in demand, or disruptions due to extreme weather, enabling stakeholders to respond proactively rather than reactively.

Supply chain optimization is a key area where AI enhances food system resilience. Algorithms can track the movement of agricultural products from producers to markets, identify bottlenecks, and optimize routes to reduce spoilage and waste. By forecasting supply and demand fluctuations, AI helps stabilize prices and ensure consistent food availability, even when external shocks occur.

AI also supports adaptive management in agriculture, allowing producers to adjust planting schedules, crop choices, and input use based on evolving conditions. In livestock systems, AI-driven monitoring tools can detect signs of disease or stress early, improving animal health and productivity. These advances are critical for maintaining stable food supplies as climate variability increases.

Food safety and quality assurance benefit as well. AI systems can analyze data from sensors, inspections, and consumer feedback to detect contamination, fraud, or quality issues at multiple stages in the supply chain. Rapid identification and response help protect public health and reduce economic losses.

Policy-makers and humanitarian organizations use AI to map food insecurity hotspots, target interventions, and design strategies that strengthen system-wide resilience. As global challenges become more complex and interconnected, AI's capacity to process information and support rapid, adaptive decision-making becomes increasingly valuable.

By supporting efficiency, adaptability, and transparency throughout food systems, AI is equipping societies to meet current and future food security challenges, making food systems more resilient and responsive in a changing world.

6.6 Chapter Summary

This chapter examined the transformative impact of AI on agriculture, land management, and food system resilience in the context of climate change. The discussion began with precision agriculture, where AI enables targeted management of crops, pests, and yields by integrating data from sensors, satellite imagery, and historical records. These advances help farmers optimize inputs, increase productivity, and reduce environmental impact.

Soil health assessment and management were highlighted as key areas where AI analyzes diverse datasets to monitor soil conditions, predict potential problems, and guide regenerative practices. By supporting real-time and site-specific decisions, AI helps maintain soil fertility, reduce degradation, and promote long-term sustainability.

Land use change monitoring and prevention were addressed, focusing on how AI processes geospatial and sensor data to detect and forecast shifts in land cover. These tools provide early warnings and inform planning, supporting efforts to limit habitat loss and encourage sustainable land use.

Deforestation detection and biodiversity conservation were explored as critical elements for maintaining ecosystem services and mitigating emissions. AI-driven monitoring and predictive modeling enable rapid detection of illegal activities, identification of key habitats, and the design of effective conservation strategies.

Food system resilience was discussed in terms of how AI supports adaptive planning, supply chain optimization, food safety, and risk management across the entire food value chain. AI enhances the ability of stakeholders to anticipate disruptions, respond to changing conditions, and safeguard food security in the face of climate variability.

Collectively, the applications covered in this chapter illustrate the vast potential of AI to support more sustainable, productive, and resilient agricultural and land systems. Through improved data analysis, real-time monitoring, and adaptive management, AI is helping to future-proof food production and ecosystem health in a rapidly changing world.

Chapter 7: AI for Urban Climate Solutions

Chapter 7 examines the transformative potential of AI in shaping climate solutions for cities—the epicenters of population, resource use, and climate risk. As urban areas face growing pressures from heatwaves, pollution, flooding, and infrastructure demands, AI is providing city leaders and planners with powerful tools to design, manage, and adapt urban environments for greater resilience and sustainability. This chapter explores the applications of AI in smart city design, urban heat island mitigation, air quality monitoring, and disaster response, as well as the optimization of transport and mobility systems. By leveraging real-time data and advanced analytics, AI helps cities anticipate challenges, coordinate adaptive strategies, and engage communities in participatory planning. These innovations are essential for creating healthier, more efficient, and climate-resilient urban spaces that can thrive in the face of an uncertain future.

7.1 Smart City Design for Climate Resilience

Designing cities for climate resilience is increasingly urgent as urban populations grow and the impacts of climate change intensify. AI is central to the evolution of smart cities, enabling planners and decision-makers to design, monitor, and adapt urban environments for sustainability, efficiency, and risk reduction.

Smart city design harnesses data from an array of sources, including sensors, satellite imagery, traffic systems, weather stations, and utility networks. AI algorithms analyze this information to provide a holistic, real-time picture of how cities function and respond to climate-related stresses. For example, AI can simulate the effects of heatwaves, heavy rainfall, or rising sea levels on urban infrastructure and populations, allowing planners to test and refine resilience strategies before implementing them.

Urban design decisions are increasingly informed by AI-driven models that optimize land use, transportation networks, and green space distribution. These models help identify the best locations for parks, water bodies, and vegetation to cool cities, manage stormwater, and enhance biodiversity. By forecasting the impacts of new developments or infrastructure projects, AI supports adaptive planning that anticipates future climate risks rather than simply reacting to them.

AI also enables integrated management of city systems, such as energy, water, and waste. Automated controls can optimize building operations, public lighting, and transportation flows to reduce emissions, conserve resources, and maintain essential services during extreme events. In emergencies, AI-powered systems can coordinate evacuations, manage emergency services, and communicate targeted alerts to residents, enhancing the city's capacity to respond to disasters.

Community engagement is another key benefit. AI-driven platforms support participatory planning by collecting and analyzing feedback from citizens, ensuring that urban resilience measures reflect local needs and priorities. These tools promote transparency, build trust, and foster collaboration between residents, businesses, and authorities.

Smart city design for climate resilience is not a one-size-fits-all solution. AI makes it possible to tailor strategies to the unique challenges and opportunities of each city, creating adaptable, efficient, and sustainable urban environments. By integrating advanced analytics, real-time monitoring, and community participation, AI is helping cities become more livable, robust, and prepared for an uncertain climate future.

7.2 Urban Heat Island Mapping and Mitigation

Urban heat islands (UHIs) occur when cities experience significantly higher temperatures than surrounding rural areas due to dense development, limited vegetation, and heat-absorbing surfaces like concrete and asphalt. This phenomenon exacerbates the impacts of heatwaves, increases energy demand for cooling, and worsens air pollution—posing health risks to urban populations. AI is becoming a crucial tool for mapping UHIs and designing effective mitigation strategies.

AI-driven UHI mapping utilizes data from satellites, airborne sensors, weather stations, and ground-based thermometers to create detailed temperature maps across cities. ML algorithms process these datasets to identify hotspots, analyze patterns of heat distribution, and track how UHIs evolve over time. These maps reveal how factors such as building density, land use, surface materials, and vegetation influence local temperatures, providing urban planners with actionable insights.

With a clear picture of UHI patterns, AI can recommend targeted interventions to cool urban environments. Algorithms can model the effects of increasing tree cover, installing green roofs, replacing dark surfaces with reflective materials, and enhancing water features. By simulating various scenarios, AI helps planners prioritize measures that offer the greatest reduction in temperature and energy use, while also considering cost and feasibility.

AI also supports the monitoring of mitigation efforts, providing real-time feedback on the effectiveness of implemented strategies. For example, after a city plants trees or deploys cool roofs, AI-powered systems can analyze sensor data and satellite images to quantify the resulting temperature changes and adjust future plans accordingly.

Community engagement is facilitated through AI platforms that visualize UHI data and solicit feedback from residents. This participatory approach ensures that mitigation measures align with local needs, enhances public awareness, and builds support for green infrastructure projects.

Addressing urban heat islands is especially important as climate change increases the frequency and severity of heatwaves. By leveraging AI for detailed mapping, predictive modeling, and adaptive management, cities can design more effective cooling strategies, reduce health risks, and create more comfortable, sustainable urban environments. These efforts contribute not only to climate resilience but also to improved quality of life for urban residents.

7.3 Air Quality Monitoring and Pollution Control

Maintaining healthy air quality in urban environments is a growing challenge as cities expand and sources of pollution multiply. Poor air quality has serious health consequences, increasing the risk of respiratory and cardiovascular diseases, and it also contributes to climate change through the emission of greenhouse gases and particulate matter. AI is transforming how cities monitor air quality and implement pollution control measures, enabling more precise, timely, and effective responses.

AI-powered air quality monitoring systems gather data from networks of sensors placed throughout a city, as well as from satellites, mobile devices, and meteorological stations. ML algorithms process this vast array of data to detect patterns, identify pollution hotspots, and track changes in air quality over time. These systems can distinguish between different types of pollutants, such as ozone, nitrogen dioxide, particulate matter, and volatile organic compounds, providing a detailed and dynamic picture of urban air quality.

Real-time analysis allows city authorities to respond quickly to pollution events. AI can trigger automated alerts when air quality deteriorates, prompting temporary restrictions on traffic or industrial activities and informing vulnerable populations about protective actions. By forecasting pollution episodes based on weather conditions, traffic patterns, and industrial emissions, AI helps city planners take proactive steps to reduce exposure and minimize health risks.

AI also supports the design and evaluation of pollution control strategies. Algorithms can simulate the effects of policy interventions, such as low-emission zones, changes in public transportation, or the adoption of green infrastructure, allowing decision-makers to prioritize the most effective measures. By continuously monitoring outcomes, AI enables cities to refine strategies over time and ensure that air quality targets are being met.

Public engagement and transparency are strengthened by AI-driven platforms that make air quality data accessible and understandable for residents. These tools empower individuals to make informed decisions about their activities and advocate for cleaner urban environments.

As cities face increasing air quality challenges linked to climate change and urbanization, AI provides the analytical power and responsiveness needed to protect public health, improve quality of life, and support sustainable urban development.

7.4 Optimizing Urban Mobility and Transport

Urban mobility and transport systems are central to the functioning and sustainability of cities, yet they are also major contributors to air pollution, greenhouse gas emissions, and traffic congestion. Optimizing these systems is a critical component of climate resilience, and AI is proving to be a transformative tool in this domain.

AI enables cities to gather and analyze vast amounts of real-time data from sources such as GPS-equipped vehicles, public transit systems, traffic cameras, and mobile applications. ML algorithms process this information to map traffic flows, identify congestion hotspots, and predict travel demand patterns throughout the day. This granular understanding allows city planners and transport authorities to design more efficient and flexible mobility networks.

AI-powered traffic management systems can dynamically adjust traffic signals, reroute vehicles, and optimize the use of road space to reduce bottlenecks and shorten travel times. These systems help decrease vehicle idling and improve the flow of buses and emergency vehicles, resulting in lower emissions and energy use. In public transport, AI models can forecast passenger demand and adapt service frequency or route planning to meet changing needs, enhancing reliability and user satisfaction.

Shared mobility services, such as bike-sharing and ride-hailing, also benefit from AI optimization. Algorithms can determine the optimal placement and distribution of shared vehicles, balancing supply and demand while minimizing empty trips. This increases access to sustainable transport options and reduces reliance on private car ownership.

AI is advancing the development and deployment of low-emission and autonomous vehicles as well. By integrating real-time data on traffic, weather, and energy availability, AI can help coordinate fleets of electric buses or driverless taxis, supporting the transition to cleaner and smarter urban mobility.

Engagement with residents is enhanced through AI-driven apps and platforms that provide personalized travel information, suggest greener routes, and promote the use of public and active transport modes. These tools encourage behavioral shifts that support broader sustainability and health objectives.

Through data-driven optimization, adaptive management, and enhanced user engagement, AI is helping cities build transport systems that are cleaner, more efficient, and better equipped to meet the challenges of urbanization and climate change.

7.5 AI in Disaster Response and Urban Adaptation Planning

Cities are increasingly vulnerable to a wide range of natural disasters, including floods, storms, heatwaves, and earthquakes—risks that are exacerbated by climate change and rapid urbanization. AI is emerging as a key asset in disaster response and adaptation planning, providing urban leaders with the tools to anticipate hazards, coordinate emergency actions, and build long-term resilience.

AI systems process diverse data streams from weather forecasts, remote sensors, social media, infrastructure networks, and historical records to create a comprehensive and real-time understanding of risk landscapes. ML algorithms can detect early warning signs of disasters, such as rising river levels or unusual weather patterns, and issue timely alerts to authorities and the public. These rapid warnings enable quicker evacuations, targeted deployment of resources, and improved situational awareness during fast-moving emergencies.

In the aftermath of disasters, AI assists response teams by analyzing aerial imagery, satellite data, and crowdsourced reports to assess damage, identify inaccessible areas, and prioritize rescue or recovery operations. Automated image analysis helps locate survivors, map debris, and estimate resource needs, all of which accelerate emergency interventions and reduce loss of life.

Urban adaptation planning also benefits from AI-driven scenario modeling and risk assessment. Planners can simulate the impacts of climate hazards under different urban development or infrastructure investment options, helping to identify vulnerabilities and design strategies that minimize future risks. For example, AI can evaluate the effectiveness of green infrastructure, updated building codes, or expanded drainage networks in reducing flood impacts.

Community engagement is enhanced by AI platforms that integrate feedback from residents, gather real-time reports during disasters, and disseminate information about safe routes, shelters, or support services. These tools promote public awareness and foster a collaborative approach to urban resilience.

As cities face an uncertain climate future, AI offers a suite of solutions for improving disaster response, accelerating recovery, and supporting strategic adaptation. By turning data into actionable insights, AI empowers urban leaders to protect people, infrastructure, and the environment from the increasing risks associated with extreme events and long-term climate change.

7.6 Chapter Summary

This chapter explored the multifaceted contributions of AI to urban climate resilience, illustrating how digital innovation is reshaping the design, operation, and management of modern cities. It began with smart city design, highlighting how AI leverages real-time data from diverse sources to inform planning, optimize land use, and anticipate the impacts of climate hazards. These capabilities help urban planners create environments that are adaptive, efficient, and capable of withstanding future climate risks.

Urban heat island mapping and mitigation were examined, emphasizing the role of AI in analyzing temperature data, identifying hotspots, and guiding targeted interventions such as tree planting or cool roof installation. These strategies lower urban temperatures, improve public health, and reduce energy demand during heatwaves.

The chapter then discussed advances in air quality monitoring and pollution control, describing how AI systems enable cities to detect pollution events, forecast air quality, and evaluate the effectiveness of mitigation measures. Enhanced data accessibility empowers both city authorities and residents to make informed decisions.

Urban mobility and transport optimization were presented as key levers for reducing emissions and congestion. AI supports dynamic traffic management, improves public transit efficiency, and fosters the integration of shared and low-emission transport solutions, all of which contribute to cleaner and more sustainable urban environments.

The use of AI in disaster response and adaptation planning was also highlighted. AI-powered early warning systems, damage assessments, and scenario modeling enable faster, more coordinated responses to emergencies and support the long-term resilience of urban communities.

Collectively, the topics in this chapter demonstrated how AI is enabling cities to respond to climate challenges with greater agility and foresight. By supporting integrated management, participatory planning, and adaptive strategies, AI is helping to build cities that are not only smarter and more efficient, but also safer, healthier, and more resilient in the face of an uncertain climate future.

Chapter 8: AI in Climate Policy, Finance, and Governance

Chapter 8 explores the expanding role of AI in shaping climate policy, driving green finance, and strengthening governance frameworks for a sustainable future. As decision-makers grapple with complex choices around mitigation, adaptation, and investment, AI offers new capabilities for data-driven climate modeling, emissions monitoring, risk assessment, and policy analysis. This chapter examines how AI supports evidence-based decision-making—enabling more accurate climate projections, transparent carbon market verification, and the development of innovative financial products. It also highlights the importance of AI-powered decision-support tools and the need for transparent, accountable governance in the design and use of these technologies. Through enhanced analytics, scenario modeling, and stakeholder engagement, AI is helping to build more responsive, effective, and inclusive systems of climate governance and finance, supporting ambitious action at local, national, and global scales.

8.1 AI-Driven Climate Modeling for Policy

Climate modeling is a foundational tool for shaping policies that address climate change, providing insights into future conditions under different scenarios. Traditional climate models are computationally intensive, require significant expertise, and often struggle with uncertainty due to the vast complexity of Earth's systems. AI is now transforming climate modeling, making it more accessible, flexible, and informative for policymakers.

AI-driven climate modeling leverages ML and data analytics to process enormous volumes of climate data, including temperature records, greenhouse gas concentrations, ocean currents, land use changes, and satellite observations. ML algorithms can identify hidden patterns, relationships, and feedbacks in these data that traditional models might miss. This enables the development of more accurate and detailed climate projections at local, regional, and global scales.

One of the main advantages of AI is its ability to quickly run multiple simulations across a wide range of variables and scenarios. Policymakers can use these models to explore the likely outcomes of different policy choices—such as emissions reductions, renewable energy adoption, or land management changes—and assess their potential impacts on temperature, precipitation, sea level, and extreme weather events. By rapidly testing and refining scenarios, AI helps decision-makers understand risks, trade-offs, and co-benefits, leading to more robust and adaptive policies.

AI also supports downscaling, translating broad climate projections into actionable information for specific communities, industries, or infrastructure projects. This capability allows local authorities and businesses to develop targeted adaptation and mitigation strategies that are tailored to their unique vulnerabilities and needs.

In addition, AI models can continually learn and improve as new data becomes available, increasing the relevance and reliability of climate information over time. Automated data integration and real-time analysis enable policymakers to monitor evolving conditions, evaluate the effectiveness of interventions, and adjust strategies as needed.

By making climate modeling faster, more precise, and more responsive to policy needs, AI empowers governments, businesses, and civil society to make better-informed decisions in the face of uncertainty. This approach accelerates the development of effective, evidence-based climate policies that are essential for building resilient and sustainable futures.

8.2 Carbon Market Monitoring and Verification

Carbon markets have become an essential mechanism for incentivizing emissions reductions and channeling investment into climate mitigation efforts. The effectiveness and credibility of these markets rely on accurate monitoring, reporting, and verification of emissions and offsets. AI is playing a transformative role in enhancing transparency, reliability, and efficiency throughout the carbon market value chain.

AI-powered systems integrate data from satellites, ground-based sensors, industrial monitoring equipment, and registries to create a comprehensive, real-time picture of emissions from various sectors and activities. ML algorithms can detect anomalies, identify potential cases of double-counting, and distinguish between genuine emissions reductions and false claims. This capability reduces the risk of fraud and increases confidence among buyers, sellers, regulators, and investors.

Verification is a critical component of carbon markets, ensuring that reported reductions are real, additional, and permanent. AI automates the verification process by analyzing large datasets to validate project performance, track carbon credits, and confirm adherence to standards and protocols. For example, AI can process satellite imagery to confirm whether a reforestation project is maintaining tree cover over time, or use sensor data to verify the operational status of methane capture equipment at landfills.

AI also enhances market transparency by providing accessible and up-to-date information on project locations, credit issuance, and transaction histories. Digital platforms powered by AI can present this information in user-friendly dashboards, supporting due diligence, risk assessment, and decision-making for all market participants. Automated alerts and reporting tools help regulators enforce compliance and respond quickly to irregularities or potential market manipulation.

The integration of AI into carbon market monitoring and verification also supports scalability, enabling markets to grow rapidly while maintaining integrity. By reducing administrative burdens and improving accuracy, AI lowers costs for participants and encourages broader adoption of carbon pricing mechanisms.

As carbon markets evolve to play an even greater role in global climate action, AI-driven monitoring and verification are helping to ensure that these systems deliver real, measurable, and lasting emissions reductions. By increasing trust and accountability, AI is supporting the transition to a low-carbon economy and the achievement of ambitious climate targets.

8.3 AI for Green Finance and Risk Assessment

Green finance plays a pivotal role in accelerating the transition to a low-carbon, climate-resilient economy by directing capital toward sustainable projects and technologies. However, assessing the risks and impacts of investments in a rapidly changing climate is a complex task. AI is enhancing the effectiveness of green finance by providing more accurate, timely, and granular analysis of both environmental and financial risks.

AI-driven platforms can process massive and diverse datasets from sources such as climate models, financial markets, company disclosures, satellite imagery, and social media. ML algorithms analyze these inputs to evaluate the environmental performance of investments, identify trends, and forecast future risks or opportunities. This allows investors, asset managers, and lenders to make more informed decisions about where to allocate capital for maximum impact and minimum risk.

One key application of AI in green finance is the assessment of climate-related financial risks. AI systems can model how physical risks—such as extreme weather, droughts, floods, or sea level rise—may affect the value of assets, infrastructure, or portfolios. They can also evaluate transition risks, including changes in regulations, technology adoption, or market preferences that could impact companies or sectors over time. These insights help financial institutions align their strategies with sustainability goals and regulatory requirements.

AI enhances due diligence and monitoring by automatically screening investments for compliance with green standards, sustainability benchmarks, and environmental, social, and governance (ESG) criteria. By detecting inconsistencies or greenwashing in disclosures and reports, AI supports transparency and accountability in sustainable finance.

Furthermore, AI can facilitate the development of innovative financial products such as green bonds, sustainability-linked loans, and blended finance solutions. By evaluating project viability, environmental impact, and credit risk, AI helps structure investments that mobilize private capital for climate action.

Regulators and policymakers benefit as well, using AI-powered analytics to monitor market trends, assess systemic risks, and design policies that incentivize sustainable investment.

As the need for climate-smart capital allocation grows, AI is becoming indispensable in green finance and risk assessment. By delivering more robust analytics, improving transparency, and supporting innovation, AI helps scale up investment in solutions that drive progress toward climate resilience and sustainability.

8.4 Decision-Support Tools for Policy and Regulation

Developing effective climate policy and regulation requires robust, timely, and actionable information to guide complex decision-making. AI is revolutionizing decision-support tools, empowering policymakers and regulators to analyze vast datasets, simulate policy outcomes, and respond flexibly to changing conditions.

AI-driven decision-support systems integrate data from multiple sources, including climate models, economic indicators, demographic statistics, and environmental monitoring networks. ML algorithms process these inputs to identify trends, forecast future scenarios, and assess the potential impacts of various policy options. This enables decision-makers to understand the likely consequences of regulatory choices—such as emissions limits, incentives for clean energy, or adaptation investments—before enacting them.

Scenario analysis is a core feature of AI-powered tools. Policymakers can test the effects of different interventions across sectors and time horizons, exploring trade-offs between economic growth, social equity, and environmental protection. For example, AI models can estimate how carbon pricing might influence industry behavior, how renewable energy mandates affect grid stability, or how adaptation policies could reduce vulnerability in coastal communities. By presenting these scenarios visually and interactively, AI makes complex data accessible and actionable.

AI also supports real-time policy monitoring and evaluation. As new data becomes available, AI systems can track progress toward policy goals, identify emerging challenges, and recommend mid-course adjustments. Automated reporting and analytics increase transparency and accountability, supporting evidence-based governance and continuous improvement.

Stakeholder engagement benefits as well. AI-enabled platforms can synthesize feedback from citizens, businesses, and advocacy groups, providing policymakers with a comprehensive understanding of public sentiment and concerns. This fosters more inclusive and responsive regulation, aligning policies with societal needs.

Regulators use AI to detect non-compliance, fraud, or unintended consequences in real time, enhancing enforcement and minimizing risks. Automated alerts and compliance checks streamline oversight and reduce administrative burdens.

By equipping policymakers and regulators with powerful analytics, visualization, and simulation tools, AI is strengthening climate governance. These decision-support systems enable more informed, adaptive, and transparent policy development, helping ensure that climate actions are effective, efficient, and responsive to an evolving world.

8.5 Transparency and Accountability in AI Governance

As AI becomes central to climate policy and regulation, ensuring transparency and accountability in its development and application is increasingly important. The effectiveness of AI in supporting climate action depends not only on its technical capabilities but also on the trust it inspires among policymakers, stakeholders, and the broader public.

Transparency in AI governance begins with clear documentation of how algorithms are designed, trained, and validated. Policymakers and regulators must be able to understand the logic behind AI-driven decisions, including the data sources used, the assumptions made, and the limitations of the models. Open access to algorithms, methodologies, and data—where appropriate—allows independent experts to scrutinize and verify results, strengthening the credibility of AI-supported policies.

Explainability is another key component of transparency. Complex ML models, especially deep learning systems, can sometimes function as "black boxes," making it difficult to interpret their decisions. Developing explainable AI techniques helps demystify these systems, providing insights into how specific outcomes or recommendations are generated. This fosters greater understanding, enables users to challenge or question results, and supports more informed decision-making.

Accountability mechanisms are necessary to assign responsibility for the outcomes of AI-driven actions. This includes establishing clear roles for data providers, algorithm developers, policymakers, and regulators. If an AI system produces biased or harmful results, accountability frameworks should provide pathways for recourse, correction, and compensation. Regular audits and impact assessments ensure that AI systems are performing as intended and that unintended consequences are identified and addressed promptly.

Ethical standards play a crucial role in maintaining both transparency and accountability. Principles such as fairness, inclusivity, and respect for privacy must be embedded in the design and deployment of AI tools for climate governance. This includes protecting sensitive data, minimizing bias, and ensuring that marginalized or vulnerable groups are not disproportionately affected by AI-driven decisions.

Public engagement is essential for building trust in AI-supported governance. Making information accessible, encouraging feedback, and involving stakeholders in the development and oversight of AI systems help align these technologies with societal values and needs.

By prioritizing transparency and accountability, AI governance can support the development of climate policies that are trusted, equitable, and effective. These safeguards are critical for realizing the full potential of AI as a tool for good in the global response to climate change.

8.6 Chapter Summary

This chapter explored the expanding role of AI in shaping climate policy, advancing green finance, and strengthening governance frameworks. The discussion began with AI-driven climate modeling, highlighting how ML enables more detailed, flexible, and actionable projections. These advances help policymakers understand the impacts of different scenarios, design adaptive strategies, and develop targeted policies at both global and local scales.

The chapter then examined the use of AI in carbon market monitoring and verification, showing how automated data analysis and remote sensing improve the credibility, transparency, and scalability of emissions trading systems. These innovations ensure that carbon markets deliver real, measurable emissions reductions and foster trust among all stakeholders.

Green finance and risk assessment were presented as areas where AI processes large and diverse datasets to evaluate environmental and financial risks, detect greenwashing, and support innovative sustainable investment products. By delivering more robust analytics, AI helps mobilize capital for climate action and guides investment toward projects with meaningful environmental benefits.

Attention was also given to decision-support tools for policy and regulation. AI-powered platforms allow policymakers to simulate the outcomes of different interventions, monitor progress in real time, and engage with stakeholders to create more responsive and effective climate policies.

The chapter concluded by emphasizing the importance of transparency and accountability in AI governance. Clear documentation, explainability, ethical standards, and stakeholder involvement are essential for building trust in AI-driven decisions and minimizing risks.

Collectively, these applications show how AI is transforming the landscape of climate policy, finance, and governance. By providing deeper insights, streamlining oversight, and supporting fair, evidence-based decision-making, AI is equipping society with the tools needed for ambitious and credible climate action in a rapidly changing world.

Chapter 9: Challenges, Risks, and Ethical Dimensions

Chapter 9 addresses the critical challenges, risks, and ethical considerations that arise as AI becomes more deeply embedded in climate adaptation and mitigation efforts. While AI offers immense promise for accelerating climate action, its deployment also brings complex questions related to data privacy, algorithmic bias, social inclusion, and environmental impact. This chapter explores concerns over energy use and emissions from AI systems, the need for algorithmic transparency and explainability, and the importance of robust governance and regulatory frameworks. It also examines the societal risks associated with employment disruption, the potential misuse of AI, and the risk of deepening inequalities. By foregrounding these issues, the chapter underscores the necessity of proactive, ethical, and inclusive approaches to AI development and deployment—ensuring that digital innovation serves the public good and supports a fair, sustainable, and resilient climate transition for all.

9.1 Data Privacy, Bias, and Inclusion

As AI becomes more deeply embedded in climate adaptation and mitigation efforts, the ethical challenges of data privacy, algorithmic bias, and social inclusion demand careful attention. Addressing these issues is essential for ensuring that AI-driven solutions are not only effective, but also fair and trustworthy.

Data privacy is a major concern as AI systems often require vast amounts of information from sensors, satellites, personal devices, and administrative records. These datasets can include sensitive details about individuals, communities, or critical infrastructure. Without strong safeguards, the misuse or unauthorized access of such data could lead to breaches of confidentiality, discrimination, or even physical risks. It is essential to implement strict data governance policies, including anonymization, encryption, and access controls, to protect personal and sensitive information.

Transparency about what data is collected, how it is used, and who has access builds public trust and encourages broader participation in AI-driven climate initiatives.

Bias in AI algorithms is another significant risk. If training data reflects historical inequalities, incomplete coverage, or systemic prejudices, AI models may perpetuate or amplify these biases in their outputs. For example, predictive tools for disaster response or resource allocation could inadvertently overlook marginalized communities or provide unequal benefits. Regular audits, diverse data sources, and inclusive development teams help identify and address these issues, promoting more equitable results.

Inclusion is critical for realizing the full potential of AI in climate action. This means ensuring that the benefits of AI technologies reach underserved and vulnerable groups, such as low-income populations, indigenous communities, or those in regions with limited digital infrastructure. Engaging diverse stakeholders throughout the design, implementation, and evaluation phases helps tailor solutions to local needs and avoid one-size-fits-all approaches that may not be effective or fair.

Promoting inclusion also involves bridging the digital divide through investments in education, training, and infrastructure. As AI becomes a central tool in climate governance, building local capacity ensures that all communities have the opportunity to shape, use, and benefit from these technologies.

By prioritizing data privacy, addressing algorithmic bias, and fostering inclusion, climate-focused AI can serve as a force for equity and empowerment, supporting sustainable solutions that protect both people and the planet.

9.2 Energy Use and Emissions from AI

While AI offers significant promise for advancing climate adaptation and mitigation, the development and operation of AI systems themselves consume energy and contribute to greenhouse gas emissions. As AI models become more complex and data-intensive, it is important to examine and address their environmental footprint to ensure that climate solutions do not unintentionally exacerbate the problem they aim to solve.

Training advanced ML models—particularly deep learning networks—requires substantial computational power. Large data centers, which house the servers and infrastructure for training and running AI algorithms, use significant amounts of electricity for both processing and cooling. Depending on the energy mix of the region, this electricity use can result in substantial carbon emissions. For example, training a single large language model or image recognition system can generate as much CO_2 as several cars over their lifetimes if powered by fossil fuels.

Operational emissions also arise from the everyday use of AI models in applications like real-time monitoring, optimization, or automated decision-making. While these tasks may use less energy than initial training, their continuous operation across thousands of devices and platforms adds up. As AI applications become more widespread— embedded in everything from smart grids to personal devices—their aggregate energy demand and climate impact increase.

Addressing these challenges requires a multi-faceted approach. Data centers can be made more energy-efficient through improved hardware design, cooling systems, and the use of renewable energy sources. Optimizing algorithms to require fewer computations, reducing redundancy, and selecting less resource-intensive models can also lower energy use. Research into "green AI" emphasizes developing techniques and best practices that minimize the energy footprint of both AI development and deployment.

Transparency is essential in understanding and managing AI's environmental impact. Disclosing the energy use and emissions associated with AI projects helps researchers, companies, and policymakers make informed choices and prioritize sustainable solutions.

By proactively addressing the energy and emissions impacts of AI, the climate community can ensure that digital innovation is aligned with broader sustainability goals. Responsible development and deployment of AI technologies support the creation of net-positive climate solutions that advance progress without adding to the global emissions burden.

9.3 Algorithmic Transparency and Explainability

As AI becomes more integrated into climate adaptation and mitigation strategies, the concepts of algorithmic transparency and explainability have gained critical importance. AI systems are often complex and operate in ways that are not immediately understandable to users, policymakers, or affected communities. Ensuring that these systems are transparent and their decisions are explainable is essential for building trust, facilitating oversight, and enabling responsible use.

Algorithmic transparency refers to the openness with which information about AI models, their design, data sources, and functioning is shared. When algorithms are transparent, stakeholders can scrutinize the logic and assumptions behind predictions or recommendations, assess their reliability, and identify potential sources of error or bias. Transparency also makes it possible to compare different models and select the most appropriate one for a given context, particularly in high-stakes climate applications such as disaster response, energy management, or resource allocation.

Explainability goes a step further by making AI decisions and outputs understandable to non-expert users. Many modern AI systems, particularly those using deep learning, function as "black boxes"—they can deliver accurate results but provide little insight into how those results are generated. Explainable AI techniques address this challenge by breaking down decisions into understandable components, highlighting key variables, and providing reasons for specific recommendations. This empowers users to interrogate AI outputs, question unusual findings, and make more informed decisions.

Ensuring transparency and explainability is especially important in climate-related applications, where decisions may affect public safety, resource distribution, or regulatory compliance. For instance, if an AI model recommends prioritizing one community over another for disaster relief or infrastructure investment, it is vital to understand why and to ensure the reasoning is fair and justifiable.

Developing transparent and explainable AI involves a combination of technical, organizational, and policy measures. Open-source models, comprehensive documentation, user-friendly visualizations, and regulatory standards all contribute to making AI systems more accessible and accountable.

By prioritizing algorithmic transparency and explainability, the climate community can harness the power of AI while maintaining public trust and upholding principles of fairness, ethics, and democratic oversight. These efforts ensure that AI supports—not undermines—responsible and effective climate action.

9.4 Governance Frameworks and Regulatory Needs

The widespread adoption of AI in climate adaptation and mitigation raises important questions about governance and regulation. Establishing clear frameworks is essential to ensure that AI is developed, deployed, and used in ways that are ethical, effective, and aligned with societal values and climate objectives.

Effective governance frameworks define the roles and responsibilities of different actors, including developers, operators, regulators, policymakers, and affected communities. These frameworks provide guidelines for best practices in data collection, model development, risk assessment, and ongoing monitoring. By setting standards for transparency, fairness, privacy, and security, governance frameworks help safeguard against misuse and unintended consequences.

Regulatory needs are evolving as AI technologies advance and become more embedded in critical climate-related systems. Regulations may address issues such as data privacy, algorithmic bias, environmental impacts, and accountability for AI-driven decisions. For example, rules can require that organizations disclose the data sources and methodologies used in AI models, regularly audit outcomes for bias, and report the energy use and emissions associated with AI systems.

International collaboration is increasingly important as AI applications and climate challenges cross borders. Harmonizing regulatory approaches helps prevent loopholes, promotes best practices, and supports interoperability of systems and data. Multilateral institutions, such as the United Nations, can play a key role in facilitating dialogue, setting global standards, and fostering cooperation.

Stakeholder engagement is central to robust AI governance. Involving communities, civil society organizations, industry, and academia in the development and oversight of AI regulations ensures that diverse perspectives are considered and that policies reflect the needs and concerns of those affected. Participatory approaches also help build public trust and legitimacy.

Adaptive governance is another essential feature, allowing regulations to evolve alongside technological advances and emerging risks. Periodic reviews, flexible standards, and the incorporation of new evidence help ensure that governance remains relevant and effective as both AI and climate challenges develop.

By establishing strong governance frameworks and responsive regulatory systems, society can maximize the benefits of AI for climate action while minimizing risks. Thoughtful, inclusive, and adaptive approaches to governance are fundamental for harnessing AI as a force for good in the pursuit of climate resilience and sustainability.

9.5 Societal Risks: Employment, Misuse, Inequality

The rapid deployment of AI in climate adaptation and mitigation brings not only opportunities, but also significant societal risks. Addressing the potential impacts on employment, the dangers of misuse, and the risk of widening inequalities is essential to ensure that AI supports an equitable transition to a sustainable future.

One major concern is the impact of AI on employment. Automation and intelligent systems may displace workers in sectors such as manufacturing, agriculture, transportation, and energy as routine or labor-intensive tasks become increasingly digitized. While AI can create new jobs—particularly in technology development, data analysis, and maintenance—there is a risk that workers without access to reskilling opportunities may be left behind. Preparing the workforce for this transition requires proactive investment in education, vocational training, and support for lifelong learning, especially for vulnerable groups.

Misuse of AI is another important risk. AI systems can be deployed with malicious intent, used to manipulate information, circumvent environmental regulations, or engage in "greenwashing"—the practice of presenting a false impression of environmental responsibility. Weak governance and oversight may allow organizations or individuals to exploit AI for personal or commercial gain at the expense of society and the environment. Developing strong regulatory frameworks, ethical guidelines, and accountability mechanisms is critical to minimizing the risk of AI misuse in climate applications.

Inequality may be exacerbated if access to AI technologies and their benefits is unevenly distributed. High costs, limited digital infrastructure, and a lack of technical capacity may prevent low-income countries or marginalized communities from adopting AI-driven solutions. This digital divide risks concentrating the advantages of AI in wealthier regions, while those most vulnerable to climate impacts are left with fewer resources and tools for adaptation or mitigation. Promoting digital inclusion, open access to data, and international cooperation can help bridge these gaps and ensure more equitable outcomes.

Social risks related to employment, misuse, and inequality must be carefully managed as AI becomes more integral to climate action. Engaging stakeholders, fostering transparent and inclusive governance, and investing in human capital are all essential steps in ensuring that AI-driven solutions contribute to social and environmental well-being for all.

9.6 Chapter Summary

This chapter addressed the key challenges and risks associated with integrating AI into climate adaptation and mitigation. It began with the issue of data privacy, bias, and inclusion, emphasizing the importance of safeguarding sensitive information, preventing algorithmic discrimination, and ensuring that the benefits of AI are accessible to all communities. Ethical data governance and inclusive development practices are necessary for building trust and equity in climate-focused AI applications.

The discussion then turned to the environmental footprint of AI, highlighting the energy consumption and emissions linked to developing and deploying advanced models. Strategies for improving data center efficiency, optimizing algorithms, and prioritizing "green AI" were presented as ways to align digital innovation with climate goals.

Algorithmic transparency and explainability were explored as essential elements for responsible AI use. By making AI models and decisions more understandable to users, these practices foster oversight, accountability, and public confidence, particularly in high-stakes climate contexts.

Governance frameworks and regulatory needs were examined, with a focus on setting standards for transparency, fairness, privacy, and adaptive oversight. The importance of international collaboration and stakeholder engagement was underscored to ensure that regulations remain relevant and effective as AI technologies and climate risks evolve.

Societal risks—including impacts on employment, potential misuse, and the exacerbation of inequality—were also discussed. Preparing workers for technological change, preventing malicious uses of AI, and promoting digital inclusion are crucial steps to ensure that AI-driven climate solutions are fair and broadly beneficial.

Taken together, the topics in this chapter highlight the necessity of proactive, ethical, and inclusive approaches to AI governance. Addressing these challenges is fundamental for unlocking the full potential of AI to support sustainable, just, and resilient climate action.

Chapter 10: The Future of AI in Climate Adaptation and Mitigation

Chapter 10 looks ahead to the evolving landscape of AI in climate adaptation and mitigation, highlighting both emerging opportunities and the essential requirements for responsible progress. As technological innovation accelerates, next-generation AI—combined with advancements in fields like quantum computing, robotics, and advanced sensing—promises to expand what is possible in climate action. This chapter explores the importance of interdisciplinary collaboration, investment in skills and capacity, and the global scaling of AI-driven solutions to ensure that benefits are equitably shared. It also discusses the need for long-term vision, global cooperation, and inclusive governance to navigate the uncertainties and risks of the coming decades. By focusing on adaptability, access, and ethical stewardship, Chapter 10 charts a path for AI to become a cornerstone of ambitious, just, and resilient climate action worldwide.

10.1 Next-Generation AI and Emerging Technologies

The pace of technological advancement is accelerating, and next-generation AI is set to play an even greater role in climate adaptation and mitigation. Emerging AI technologies—often combined with breakthroughs in fields such as robotics, quantum computing, and advanced sensing—are opening up new frontiers for how societies respond to climate challenges.

One promising area is the development of more efficient, scalable, and self-learning AI models. Advances in edge computing allow AI systems to process data and make decisions closer to where it is generated—such as on farms, in factories, or within smart city infrastructure—reducing latency, energy use, and dependence on centralized data centers. This increases the resilience and flexibility of climate solutions, especially in remote or resource-constrained regions.

Quantum computing, though still in its early stages, holds the potential to dramatically accelerate the processing of complex climate models, optimization problems, and molecular simulations for new materials or energy systems. When integrated with AI, quantum technology could enable breakthroughs in forecasting, emissions reduction, and resource management that are currently beyond reach with classical computing.

Robotics and autonomous systems are also evolving rapidly, with AI-powered drones, robots, and vehicles increasingly used for environmental monitoring, disaster response, ecosystem restoration, and precision agriculture. These systems can collect high-resolution data, perform tasks in hazardous conditions, and support adaptation efforts where human intervention is limited or dangerous.

Advanced sensing and the IoT are expanding the data available for AI to analyze. Networks of connected sensors can monitor environmental conditions, track changes in infrastructure, and support real-time decision-making for resource use, emissions, and risk management. This growing web of smart devices forms the backbone of responsive and adaptive climate solutions.

Interdisciplinary convergence is a hallmark of next-generation AI. The integration of digital twins, blockchain for transparent data management, and synthetic biology for developing climate-resilient crops or materials exemplifies how multiple emerging technologies can reinforce each other's impact.

By embracing next-generation AI and related innovations, the climate community can unlock new capabilities, accelerate the development of transformative solutions, and build systems that are more adaptive, efficient, and sustainable in the face of growing climate risks.

10.2 Interdisciplinary Collaboration and Climate-AI Integration

Tackling the complex and interconnected challenges of climate change requires the integration of diverse knowledge, skills, and perspectives. Interdisciplinary collaboration is fundamental to maximizing the impact of AI in climate adaptation and mitigation, ensuring that AI solutions are robust, context-appropriate, and aligned with societal needs.

Effective climate-AI integration begins with close cooperation between climate scientists, data scientists, engineers, urban planners, policymakers, and community leaders. Climate experts contribute domain-specific knowledge about environmental systems, risks, and interventions, while AI specialists bring expertise in ML, data analysis, and algorithm development. Together, these groups can design, test, and refine AI tools that address real-world climate priorities and challenges.

Collaboration extends beyond technical fields to include social scientists, economists, ethicists, and practitioners from sectors such as health, agriculture, and energy. These perspectives help ensure that AI applications are socially equitable, economically viable, and ethically sound. Engaging with stakeholders—including vulnerable populations, indigenous communities, and local organizations— enriches the understanding of climate impacts and supports the development of solutions that are both effective and inclusive.

Interdisciplinary teams are particularly valuable in translating complex scientific findings into actionable policies, innovative business models, or practical interventions. For example, urban planners working alongside AI experts and public health officials can co-create smart city solutions that address both climate resilience and community well-being. In agriculture, collaboration between agronomists, engineers, and technology providers drives the deployment of precision farming tools tailored to local conditions.

Open data sharing, collaborative research platforms, and joint funding mechanisms support the exchange of knowledge and the scaling of best practices. Global partnerships and networks facilitate the adaptation of successful AI solutions to different geographies, climates, and social contexts.

Education and capacity building are also critical. Training programs and interdisciplinary curricula can equip the next generation of professionals with the skills needed to bridge the gap between climate science and AI technology.

Through interdisciplinary collaboration and integrated approaches, AI can be harnessed as a powerful enabler of climate action. By bringing together diverse expertise and engaging all stakeholders, society can create innovative, equitable, and scalable solutions that address the urgent challenges of climate change.

10.3 Skills, Capacity, and Education Needs

The effective use of AI in climate adaptation and mitigation depends on the availability of skilled professionals, strong institutional capacity, and accessible education pathways. As AI becomes increasingly central to climate action, investing in human capital and organizational readiness is essential to maximize its benefits and ensure equitable outcomes.

Building AI skills for climate applications requires a blend of technical and domain-specific expertise. Professionals need a solid foundation in data science, ML, programming, and statistics, as well as a deep understanding of climate science, environmental systems, and policy frameworks. Cross-disciplinary training programs, workshops, and academic courses can help bridge the gap between technical and climate-focused fields, enabling individuals to work effectively at the intersection of AI and climate action.

Capacity building extends beyond individual skills. Organizations— whether government agencies, research institutes, businesses, or NGOs—must develop the structures, processes, and cultures needed to support AI-driven solutions. This includes investing in digital infrastructure, fostering a culture of innovation and collaboration, and establishing ethical guidelines for responsible AI use. Leadership and management training should emphasize the strategic value of AI, helping decision-makers identify opportunities and risks, set priorities, and align resources for maximum impact.

Education systems at all levels play a pivotal role. Integrating AI and climate literacy into school curricula, vocational programs, and higher education ensures that the next generation is equipped to navigate and shape the rapidly evolving digital landscape. Partnerships between universities, industry, and government can support research, internships, and practical training, offering real-world experience and fostering ongoing learning.

Digital inclusion is also critical to avoid widening inequalities. Efforts should be made to make AI and climate education accessible to underrepresented groups, low-income communities, and regions with limited technological resources. Scholarships, outreach programs, and online learning platforms can expand opportunities and promote diversity in the climate-AI workforce.

By investing in skills, capacity, and education, society can unlock the full potential of AI for climate resilience and sustainability. A well-trained, diverse, and adaptable workforce—supported by strong institutions and inclusive education systems—is fundamental to advancing AI-powered climate solutions and ensuring they serve the needs of all communities.

10.4 Scaling Solutions Globally and Ensuring Access

Expanding the benefits of AI for climate adaptation and mitigation requires more than technological innovation—it demands strategies to scale successful solutions globally and ensure equitable access for all. Addressing climate change is a worldwide challenge, and AI-driven tools must be designed and deployed in ways that reach diverse geographies, economies, and communities.

Scaling AI solutions involves adapting technologies and practices developed in one context to work effectively in others. This may require modifying algorithms to account for local data availability, climate conditions, infrastructure, and regulatory environments. Collaborative networks of governments, research institutions, and the private sector can facilitate knowledge transfer, technical assistance, and the sharing of best practices across borders. Open-source AI platforms and publicly accessible datasets lower barriers to entry, enabling innovators in low- and middle-income countries to tailor and implement tools for their own needs.

Ensuring access goes beyond technology transfer. It requires targeted investment in digital infrastructure—such as broadband connectivity, reliable power, and data centers—in underserved regions. Support for local capacity building, including training and education, empowers communities to adopt, maintain, and evolve AI solutions independently. Partnerships with local organizations, NGOs, and community leaders help ensure that AI applications reflect local priorities, cultures, and values.

Financial mechanisms play a critical role in scaling and access. International funding, grants, and blended finance models can support pilot projects, infrastructure development, and capacity-building efforts in resource-limited settings. Donor agencies, multilateral banks, and philanthropic organizations can leverage their resources to bridge funding gaps and de-risk investment in frontier markets.

Policy frameworks must also encourage responsible scaling and access. Governments and international bodies can establish standards for data sharing, interoperability, and ethical AI deployment, while protecting privacy and promoting inclusivity. Encouraging open collaboration and avoiding restrictive proprietary practices help prevent technological lock-in and foster innovation.

By focusing on global scaling and equitable access, the climate and AI communities can ensure that digital innovation benefits all people and regions—not just a privileged few. Empowering countries and communities to harness AI for climate resilience is essential for achieving the collective ambition of a more sustainable, adaptive, and climate-secure world.

10.5 Long-Term Visions and Global Cooperation

Addressing climate change through AI requires a long-term perspective and unprecedented levels of global cooperation. The challenges of climate adaptation and mitigation are interconnected and transboundary, demanding collective action that transcends individual sectors, nations, and regions. A forward-looking vision for AI in climate action must prioritize not only technological advancement, but also shared responsibility, inclusivity, and sustainable development for all.

A long-term vision recognizes that climate change will continue to evolve over decades, affecting societies, economies, and ecosystems in ways that are often unpredictable. AI-powered climate solutions must be designed for flexibility and resilience, capable of adapting to new knowledge, shifting conditions, and emerging risks. This means investing in research and development, fostering open scientific exchange, and encouraging innovation across disciplines. Establishing "living" platforms that can evolve over time helps ensure that AI tools remain relevant and effective as the climate and technology landscapes change.

Global cooperation is vital for scaling up successful AI-driven solutions and addressing disparities in capacity and access. International partnerships among governments, research institutions, businesses, and civil society organizations create pathways for knowledge sharing, resource pooling, and coordinated action. Multilateral forums—such as the United Nations, the Intergovernmental Panel on Climate Change (IPCC), and global innovation networks—play a key role in harmonizing standards, setting collective targets, and fostering a spirit of solidarity.

Joint investment in infrastructure, open data platforms, and capacity-building initiatives supports the diffusion of AI technologies and best practices to countries and communities most in need. International funding mechanisms, technology transfer agreements, and collaborative research projects can bridge gaps in expertise and resources.

Long-term visions also require inclusive governance that elevates the voices of all stakeholders, especially those most affected by climate change and technological change. Transparent, participatory decision-making ensures that AI-powered climate strategies are equitable and responsive to diverse needs.

By aligning technological progress with shared values, ethical principles, and global goals, the climate and AI communities can chart a course toward a sustainable, resilient, and just future. Lasting progress on climate action will depend on sustained cooperation, visionary leadership, and a commitment to leaving no one behind. AI, harnessed collectively and responsibly, can be a cornerstone of this transformative journey.

10.6 Chapter Summary

This chapter explored the future directions, opportunities, and essential requirements for harnessing AI in global climate adaptation and mitigation. It began by discussing next-generation AI and emerging technologies, emphasizing the potential of edge computing, quantum computing, robotics, and advanced sensing to accelerate innovation and enable more adaptive, efficient climate solutions.

The chapter highlighted the critical role of interdisciplinary collaboration in developing AI tools that are robust, context-sensitive, and equitable. Bringing together climate scientists, data experts, engineers, social scientists, and community stakeholders ensures that solutions are both technically sound and aligned with real-world needs.

Attention was given to the need for investment in skills, capacity, and education. Building a workforce equipped with both AI and climate expertise is fundamental for realizing the full potential of digital innovation in climate action. Inclusive education and capacity-building efforts help prevent the widening of digital divides and ensure that diverse communities can participate in and benefit from AI-driven climate strategies.

Scaling solutions globally and ensuring access were presented as key priorities. The adaptation of AI tools for different regions, the strengthening of digital infrastructure, and the development of supportive policy and financing mechanisms are necessary to achieve equitable deployment and widespread impact.

Finally, the chapter addressed the importance of long-term vision and global cooperation. Sustained international collaboration, inclusive governance, and flexible, evolving approaches are required to meet the challenges of climate change over decades to come.

Taken together, the topics in this chapter underscore the transformative power of AI—when thoughtfully developed, inclusively governed, and widely accessible—to advance ambitious, resilient, and just climate action on a global scale.

Conclusion

As we reach the conclusion of this book, it is clear that AI is poised to play a defining role in the global response to climate change.

Key Themes and Opportunities

This book has examined the vital intersection of AI and climate action, highlighting how AI is rapidly transforming adaptation and mitigation strategies across energy, industry, water, agriculture, cities, and policy. AI's ability to process complex data, forecast scenarios, optimize resource use, and automate decision-making is opening new frontiers for climate resilience and sustainability. Key opportunities include smarter integration of renewable energy, enhanced disaster prediction and response, improved monitoring and management of natural resources, and the acceleration of green finance and transparent governance. The integration of AI with emerging technologies, robust data systems, and collaborative, interdisciplinary approaches amplifies these benefits, enabling more adaptive, efficient, and equitable solutions for communities around the world. With the right vision and investment, AI can serve as a cornerstone of a climate-secure future.

Limitations and Trade-Offs

Despite its promise, the deployment of AI for climate solutions is not without limitations. AI models require significant energy, data, and computational resources, which themselves have environmental impacts. Issues of data quality, algorithmic bias, digital divides, and explainability present ongoing challenges. Trade-offs often arise between speed, precision, and inclusivity, and between centralized efficiency and local empowerment. No single technology can address the full spectrum of climate risks, and over-reliance on AI may distract from necessary structural, social, and behavioral changes.

The Imperative for Ethical, Inclusive, Global Action

Maximizing the benefits of AI for climate action requires an unwavering commitment to ethics, inclusivity, and global cooperation. AI systems must be designed and governed with fairness, transparency, and accountability at their core. This includes robust protections for privacy and data security, regular audits for bias, and open engagement with diverse stakeholders. Ensuring equitable access to AI tools and knowledge is essential to avoid deepening existing inequalities. International collaboration and policy harmonization are key to addressing transboundary risks and scaling best practices. By centering human values, societal needs, and environmental stewardship, the climate and AI communities can ensure that digital innovation uplifts all people and regions.

Final Thoughts: The Road Ahead

The journey toward climate resilience and sustainability is ongoing and requires adaptive, creative, and collective effort. AI is a powerful catalyst—but not a panacea. Its greatest promise lies in supporting informed, ethical, and collaborative action across scales and sectors. By investing in skills, infrastructure, governance, and global partnerships, societies can harness AI's potential to drive just and lasting climate solutions. The path forward is challenging, but with bold vision and shared responsibility, AI can help guide us toward a more sustainable, secure, and hopeful future.